Woman Empowered 2

Thank you for your Love & Support!! I Pray this Book Inspire you to Get your Blessings!!

Sparkle

Woman Empowered 2

Fierce, Fabulous & Free

Visionary Author Angela Lewis and Fierce, Fabulous & Free

Co-Authors; Tammie Parker; Sparkle Taneka Robertson; Rhonda Williams-Turner; P' Angela Jones; Natashah Khan; Valerie C. Thompson; Jasmine D. Milhouse; Jamaica Townsend; Keisha Grant; Wanda Leonard; Chef LaToya Larkin; Carnesha Stanton; Deborah Cooper; and Charlotte Gillespie

A & M Publishing & Productions

Publishing Company: A & M Publishing & Productions

For information contact:

contact@aandmproductions.biz
www.aandmproductions.biz

Cover artwork: by A & M Publishing & Productions

ISBN:

Printed in: The United States, First Edition

This book was produced with Pressbooks (https://pressbooks.com) and rendered with Prince.

Contents

Foreward Marissa L. Bloedoorn		ix
Fierce, Fabulous & Free: The Introduction Angela Lewis		1

Part I. Keisha Grant

1.	Dedication	5
2.	Be True to Yourself	7
3.	Biography	23

Part II. Chef LaToya Larkin

4.	Dedication	27
5.	I Earned My Glow-Up Degree from Net Worth University Chef LaToya Larkin, MBA, CCE	29
6.	Biography	43

Part III. Jasmine D. Milhouse

7.	Dedication	49
8.	Guess What, Sis? You Win!	51
9.	Biography	59

Part IV. Sparkle Taneka Robertson

10.	Dedication	63
11.	My 1% Counts and Matters	65
12.	Biography	75

Part V. Deborah Cooper

13.	Dedication	79
14.	Being the Queen That I Am!	81
15.	Biography	85

Part VI. Wanda Leonard

16.	Dedication	91
17.	The Loud Silence	93
18.	Biography	109

Part VII. Charlotte Gillespie

19.	Dedication	113
20.	Healing a Broken Heart	115
21.	Biography	123

Part VIII. Jamaica Townsend

22.	Dedication	127
23.	I am who you say I am: My Journey to finding my identity	129
24.	Biography	139

Part IX. Valerie C. Thompson

25.	Dedication	143
26.	Rise Lotus Flower	145
27.	Biography	157

Part X. P' Angela Jones

28.	Dedication	161
29.	Fierce Fabulous & Free: A Mindset	163
30.	Biography	167

Part XI. Carnesha Stanton

31.	Dedication	171
32.	Freedom From The Past!	173
33.	Biography	183

Part XII. Natashah Khan

34.	Dedication	187
35.	Free!!	189
36.	Biography	201

Part XIII. Rhonda Williams-Turner

37.	Dedication	205
38.	The Experience	207
39.	Biography	215

Part XIV. Tammie Parker

40.	Dedication	219
41.	Free To Be Me!	221
42.	Biography	225

Part XV. Angela Lewis

43.	Dedication	229
44.	Living my Life Unmuted	231
45.	Biography	235

Foreward

Marissa L. Bloedoorn

I AM A WOMAN EMPOWERED! I have watched "Dr." Angela Lewis lead countless women as well as men into a higher level of self-actualization tapping into each life, causing them to unleash and maximize their full potential in life, passion, and purpose. Lewis is a natural leader, coach, visionary, and charismatic influencer inspiring her clients, partners, and collaborators to awaken to the limitless possibilities followed by showing them the way to a life filled with purpose, to be on purpose, and with the intent to empower, educate, and equip both women and men. This is a serious season in which if you want more you have to be empowered to level up and achieve more.

Under the umbrella of "I AM A WOMAN EMPOWERED" Lewis has ignited a movement. She has created a community that is filled with love and support. Leading by example she serves with excellence, selflessness, commitment, and countlessly goes above and beyond to ensure everyone in her tribe becomes A WOMAN EMPOWERED. As I mentioned earlier, I have had the honor and pleasure of watching and participating in many of her projects to see her in action front and center empowering one at a time or as a collective. Lewis is a leader who not only takes the lead, she also empowers others to take center stage and own it by graciously stepping back for them to step forward into complete ownership of their passion, purpose, and calling. This is where you can see "I AM A WOMAN EMPOWERED" as the movement it truly is.

Each of these women are sharing their story and God's glory for their victory. We go through, but we never have to remain in our drama and the trauma that comes with it. The intent is for the reader or hearer of the story to see themselves as empowered, victorious, with their own capability of coming out of the muck and mire to walk into all God has for them. It takes courage beyond imagination to become transparent through projects like this with the hopes of freeing yourself by sharing your story and helping someone else to know he or she is not alone. There are so many who walk among us lost, depressed, abused, in pain, stuck, hopeless, low in self-worth, feeling unloved, and on the brink of committing suicide. It is stories like the stories in this edition of "I AM A WOMAN EMPOWERED" that stop someone from killing themselves, continuing to remain in unhealthy abusive relationships, to get free, to remain their faith, and destroy hopelessness, to become happy and filled with joy again. These stories are critical in turning the tide for all those that read this book from cover to cover.

You will find yourself in either one or many of the stories because if we are real with ourselves, we have all been there and done that. We have experienced the highs and lows of life and it is the rising up that inspires and empowers others to do the same. If you are looking for a home to rest your past and be empowered into your today, tomorrow, and beyond look no further. Don't stop at reading this book, you want to join the next project, become a member of the "I AM A WOMAN EMPOWERED" family, and join the MOVEMENT!

This has been an absolutely beautiful journey. I met "Dr." Lewis, many years ago and what an honor it was this past year to join the "I AM A WOMAN EMPOWERED" Movement. These are some amazing sisters, and they keep the flow real, deep, loving, compassionate, and the support again I tell you ENDLESS! This is a sisterhood that is large in size and in the heart. As the saying goes, "As the head goes, so does the body." Lewis leads with compassion, love, and a vision designed to make a mark forever on this world that cannot be erased. This is a MOVEMENT filled with LEGACY! As you read through every page, every story, and see yourself, remind yourself, "I AM A WOMAN EMPOWERED!"

Marissa L. Bloedoorn

CEO, TCS Consulting LLC

Publisher, "Own It!" Magazine & Publishing LLC

Fierce, Fabulous & Free: The Introduction

Angela Lewis

It's a Mood...a Vibe...a Mindset...a Lifestyle. It's the Standard. It's an entire elevation of consciousness. To be Fierce, Fabulous, and Free is to embody the essence of who we were created to be. Psalm 139:14 says, "I will praise You, for I am fearfully and wonderfully made. Marvelous are your works, and that my soul knoweth right well. (NKJV)

Empowerment is defined as the process of becoming stronger and more confident, especially in controlling one's life and planning one's rights. An empowered woman is one who recognizes and embraces the fullness of who she was created to be. She celebrates the intricacies within her DNA and knows that she can never be duplicated because she is the only one.....Yes...A masterpiece!

She is fiercely fearless at pursuing her dreams because she knows God has already equipped her with everything she needs. She is confident in her success because Jeremiah 29:11 says, "For I know the plans I have for you, declares the Lord, "plans to prosper you and not harm you, plans to give you hope and a future." She has faith in his word and looks towards her future, not her past. The past no longer has a hold on her because it no longer defines her. It almost destroyed her, making her weak, unsure, and doubting her worth.

The past was arrogant, playing chess to her checkers. But, it underestimated her. When the student is ready, the teacher will appear. She quietly took notes and got skilled at the assignment that she now understood. Delayed does not mean denied....she felt her strength coming back. She started gaining confidence from the daily affirmations she spoke. The lack mindset was replaced with an abundance mindset, and she started taking empowered actions. Fabulousness was awakening inside of her. Like a butterfly from the cocoon, she was Free!

A shift had occurred, and she was ready. It was time for her to know her worth and add tax! As you read this, get prepared to go on the journey with 14 women as they share their experiences on becoming Fierce, Fabulous & Free.

Visionary Author

Angela Lewis

I

Keisha Grant

1.

Dedication

Dedicated In Loving Memory to my heroes: Doris Phillips (Grandmother), Jacqueline Melson (Aunt), and Jeanette Montgomery (Aunt). Thank you for pouring into my life. I am who I am because of you. Your smiles will always shine on me. Your presence is gone by my side, but never from my heart. I love you! Rest In Peace Sisters. To my beautiful daughters: You are the wind beneath my wings. You are my motivation. I love you with every fiber in me. Thank you! To my squad of sister-friends: Queens, I do not know where I would be without you. Thank you for holding me down over the years, your everlasting support means the world to me. To my supportive organizations: Woman U, O.E.S., Al-Karim Court. 219, I am "Better Than Amazing" Thank you! To the beautiful women that have experienced trauma in their life, be bold and fearless to divorce your past. Thank you, Matthew, and A&M Publishing! To my amazing best friend: Your unconditional love is priceless! You are my rock and my balance. Thank you for your understanding and patience. The best is yet to come for us! I love you. Lastly, to my loving parents: I know my self-worth because of your love. You have helped me to find my way through life. Thank you for always supporting me! "I AM ROYALTY." Peace and Blessings!

2.

Be True to Yourself

Broken Silence: Innocence

Imagine a 10-year-old girl in the sixth grade full of life and innocence. Her dad was in the military, and her mother worked for the government. For over six years, the family lived in Europe, staying in military housing during her dad's overseas tour. The military housing was three to four stories high, with a basement at the bottom. She loved her experience in Europe because of the friendliness and the low crime rate. It was safe to leave your doors open, and no one would bother your home. She grew up as the only child in the house. Her parents raised her to be independent, and she became a latch key kid while they went to work. She would walk miles to school in the snow up to her waist. Although the walk was long, she enjoyed watching the snow. Her parents trusted her to do the chores in the house because they had trained her well. Her peers loved her at school. She had a best friend named Krystal, and they always had a fun time together. Although her parents did not care for her sleeping over at friends' houses, they trusted that she would be safe with Krystal's family.

She and Krystal were tomboys. They were not into wearing dresses and being prissy. They liked to play football with the boys and shoot marbles together. Two of their classmates stayed two buildings over from Krystal. They were all friends until the two boys snatched her in the basement and gang-raped her one day. She fought to keep her innocence. She screamed as loud as she could for help, but no one heard her. They blocked the doors as she tried to get away. It was dark, dank, and stank in this abandoned, dirty room. The darkness was so thick she could not see her hand in front of her. "HELP, HELP," she yelled!!! Her hands were bound, and their hands were over her mouth. She fought and fought. "Please do not do this," she begged. Her shirt was ripped open, and her breasts exposed. She was too young to have to experience this discomfort. Krystal could not open the door because they had it blocked, so she ran to wake her dad up to help. Once he forced the door open, the boys ran out.

She was scared and embarrassed. She trusted them. How could this happen to her? She cried and cried for the rest of the night. She begged Mr. Tony not to tell her parents because they would not let her be friends with Krystal ever again. Also, she knew her parents would be at odds with Krystal's parents because they failed to keep her safe. She promised Mr. Tony she would inform her parents when she went home, but that never happened. Instead, she lived with the pain and never confided in anyone because she was ashamed. How could she ever be able to look at herself in the mirror again? Her self-esteem was destroyed. She felt dirty, unwanted, believing no one would like her because she was damaged and worthless. She had thought of suicide to take her away from the pain she was feeling. The traumatizing experience stripped her of her innocence. She channeled her pain as she grew up by being rebellious, promiscuous, and fighting. This is her broken silence!

Empowerment: Determination

How determined are you to win when life has you bound? Who are you? Do you know your purpose in life? What are your goals? These are all the questions the young, broken girl asked when she looked in the mirror from a child to adulthood. Even though the odds were stacked against her, she did not want to be a product of her environment. She wanted more for herself than to be labeled. The troubled girl is now a woman with dreams and ambitions to do remarkable things in her life. She always wanted to be influential to other women that have experienced trauma the way she did. Whether in her personal, professional, or social relationships, confidence is required to move forward. She set the tone in her career that she is a strong black woman. Her superpower comes from the force within her soul to overcome opposition. The mirror talk she has with herself motivates her to endure whatever comes her way. Anything is possible if she can rise above the trauma in her adolescent years.

Having a passion for the healthcare industry, she desired to become a Surgical Registered Nurse. Her determination to succeed encouraged her to graduate from high school after a long struggle of rebellion. Her parents had lost faith that she would graduate on time. She managed to attend Atlanta Area Technical College to major in Certified Nursing Assistant, graduating with honors. Life was not going to defeat her. She had something to prove to those who doubted her. She enjoyed going to school because knowledge is power. Due to her passion for nursing, she wanted all the training she could get to be successful in her career. She was excited to enroll at Sanford Brown College on her educational journey, majoring in Certified Medical Assistant. No matter her age, she was determined to graduate Suma Cum Laude and be in the Top 10th Percentile of her class. Going to school had been the way she coped with the unsettling history from the past. It was a continuous effort to work on her self-esteem, but she did not let that stop her. She continued to educate herself by admitting to Clayton State University as a non-traditional student. Her major was Healthcare Management and Health Science. She graduated Cum Laude with a Bachelor of Science degree. At this point, learning had become a part of her DNA. Her tenacity pushed her to attend her alma mater, Clayton State University, to achieve a Master of Healthcare Administration. She will not quit until she conquers her goals. Her age is nothing but a number because she will get the reward in the end.

It is liberating that she is the captain of her ship and has control over her destiny. Her children are amazed at the vast amount of education she obtained. They often asked her where she gets her strength from? She comes from a lineage of strong women in her family. Her gorgeous mother has always been a diva, teaching her how to be a lady and take care of herself. Her style was truly inherited from her grandmother and mother, who loved fashion and looking good. Her strength came from the matriarchs of her family. These three beautiful sisters inspired her to think big and dream big. Her world crumbled because of the curse of cancer on her family. She watched her grandmother and two Aunts battle the deadly disease of cancer. The complications they suffered while getting cancer treatments were heartbreaking. They did not complain about their situation but fought to the very end to beat cancer. These three women are her heroes, and she is a better woman because of them. They have empowered her to keep fighting and never let anyone trick her out of her position. Strength is her name, and she will stay on her game with determination!

Racism Sucks: Survival Mode

In the midnight hours during her alone time, she would reflect on how she overcame the need for acceptance and still overcomes the pain of the past. She is adamant not to let her past life determine who she is today because the past is the past for a reason. The struggles in her life made her go over and beyond for her children. She wanted a pleasurable experience for them. Wounds heal in time, and time brings about change. Changing her mindset over her circumstances would take the shackles off her ankles. It would free her from the pain she endured to be happy in life. The more she attempted to free herself from bondage mentally, emotionally, and physically, she became trapped by racism. Prejudice was not in her DNA. Her parents raised her in a multicultural environment overseas, so she had a love for people no matter what ethnic status they were. Love saw no color in her eyes. It made her sick to know racism is more prevalent than she thought. It was survival mode for her as she became a victim of racism in the workplace.

Too often, the topic of racism is uncomfortable and creates traumatic images from our ancestors over 400 years ago. This six-letter word has suppressed us as a people and kept us mentally bound. It was mind-boggling dealing with racial conflict in 2017. Racism became more ubiquitous in her life as the days went by. It was no longer a hidden agenda or swept under the rug to hide its ugly face. Racism is as real as real can be! During her working years as a healthcare professional, racism became more frequent in her career. She tried to put the day-to-day struggle behind her and continue with life; however, the detriment of a hostile environment quickly reminded her that she was just another educated COLORED woman.

The constant reminders of no pay increases and black jokes were the daily conversations that she ignored. She had to pray to her Higher Supreme to give her patience, controlled temperance, and a bridled tongue. The only thing that got her through the day was scripture reading, the serenity prayer, and gospel music. Her favorite scripture is Isaiah 54:17, "No weapon that is formed against thee shall prosper; and every tongue that shall rise against thee in judgment thou shalt condemn. This is the heritage of the servants of the LORD, and their righteousness is of me, saith the LORD." She recited it every day to give her strength to prevail from the negative energy in her office. It seemed like the harder she worked to prove herself, the harder racism knocked her down. Her faith started to get weary. The more she prayed to God to protect her from the cruelness of racism, family substance abuse, generational cancer, and broken relationships, the more it was evident that she could not run from it.

Frequently, she would ponder why her colleagues were prejudging before they got to know her. She knew she had to co-exist with them to get her job done, believing the situation would get better as time went on. Instead, it got worse for her. Her colleagues were very disrespectful by throwing things at her and snatching things out of her hand. The presence of racism was starting to get the best of her. One of the colleagues was from Alabama, so she felt entitled to have this type of behavior towards her. It was disheartening to be treated so unjustly. She did not know how to handle this situation because she needed her job. The rejection hurt her because she loved everyone equally. Obviously, she was a threat because of her education, and they did not want her on the management team with them. Being a receptionist making $12.00 an hour was their ideal position for her. How can the color of her skin be the determining factor if she is qualified for a job or has enough education to be treated with respect?

Countless times this black woman had to second guess if she was capable of withstanding the pressure from Corporate America. She had to realize prejudice was embedded in them from childhood. Her colleagues made it known the black race is beneath their status quo or not as intelligent as a Caucasian individual. She had never dealt with the racism of this magnitude. The profession she loved had become toxic, stressful, and miserable. She remembers the troubling events of how her supervisor treated her after she graduated from college. All the arduous work she devoted to her studies and the sacrifices made to attend school did not mean anything. Her supervisor was an older Caucasian woman overseeing the Human Resources Department. She recalls her supervisor laughing insultingly in her face when she wanted another badge representing her degree credentials in Healthcare Management and Health Science.

The supervisor asked, "What are your credentials?" When she begins to tell her, she makes a joke of her degree, saying sarcastically, "BS is for bull@#$%@!" That comment crushed her enthusiasm as a new graduate. Instantly, there was a fire in her heart from the anger she had built up that wanted to lash out at her supervisor. She paused with tears in her eyes to collect her thoughts. She could not believe this was happening to her in the workplace! It was suddenly a slap in the face from her supervisor. It was inappropriate and demeaning on all levels. How dare she diminishes her degree as if she were not worthy of it! She immediately went into defensive mode to stand up for herself. If it meant being insubordinate or losing her job to voice what is morally and ethically right, that was the consequence she was willing to face.

From that moment, she prayed relentlessly to God to remove her supervisor from that position or remove her from the company. God answered her prayers. Staying faithful and trusting the process is what got her through it. The torment was over because her supervisor and the executive director resigned from their positions. God is so good! She was able to get a promotion on her job with a pay increase. She decided to remain with the company and continue to do her work to the best of her ability. Making a difference and being an effective healthcare professional was her goal. She won the battle against racism at her job. Victory, victory, victory!

Fierce: Solid as Rock

"Dear Sister"

To be a woman comes with a sense of power. Greatness is destined from the moment God created a woman to give life from her womb. Life for her was not perfect or as she expected it to be. There were plenty of bumps in the road, and she had to jump over many hurdles to get to where she is today. Her inner circle made her feel safe. She was the youngest out of her sister-friends. They all took care of each other and provided support to their children. Although she was the oldest daughter of her parent's children, she grew up in the household by herself. Her friends were sisters from another mister. They did not see each other much, but they were always a phone call away. She admired her sisters for the love they always gave to her. She looked up to them because they were free-spirited and fun to be around. Their friendship was everlasting, and the bond between all of them was solid as a rock. They had been sister friends over the decades.

She would constantly think about them and all the crazy wild things they used to do when they were younger. She could hear her mother stating, "You are going to be what you hang around." The cliché statement, "Birds of a feather flock together."

Hearing her mother's voice subconsciously made her chuckle because they all stayed in trouble or did things out of the norm. They were unapologetic beautiful black queens living their lives on the edge with NO WORRIES! She is proud of her sisters because they are fierce and doing well in life. Whenever she felt powerless and doubted her purpose, she would read an email from her Big Sister Gigi. Gigi always knew what to say to make her feel strong again. She could expect honesty coming from her no matter if the truth hurts to hear it. Gigi did not say much, but when she did speak, you better listen. She was a single parent full of wisdom. Gigi knew her better than she knew herself. Gigi's letter touched her soul. The letter reads:

"Dear Sister,

We have been friends for 20+ years. When I met you, you were a young girl on fire. You have always hungered after life and had to be the life of the party. Sister, you have never been afraid to speak your mind. You have been very outspoken ever since I have known you. Your contagious smile will light up a room, but do not get it twisted; behind that beautiful smile is a very tough-skinned woman. Sister, you are a "Go-Getter." If there is one thing I know about you, you are not afraid to step out on faith. Whether you win or lose, you will still come out on top. Sister, you have always had a strong will to succeed, and you put your best foot forward no matter what it is. All the years I have known you, you have always been incredibly supportive. Your kindness and compassion for people is who you really are. Showing unconditional love comes easy for you. Sister, you are a force to be reckoned with. Anyone that knows you knows that you have a strong will to survive. Through your struggles, up and downs, losing loved ones, you are still standing. Sister, you will always try to find a way to smile through your pain. You are an impressive mom, friend, sister, and Queen B. Also, you are innovative, creative, loving, caring, confident, fearless, productive, and not fazed by what other people say or think. Sister, you are not afraid to stand up for what you believe. You are true to yourself. As a strong black woman, you have stood the test of time. You have faced many challenges and never backed down. Little Sister, you have stayed on the course to reach your goals, and although it got tough, you never gave up. Giving up is not in your vocabulary. You own your success, and you believe in your ability to thrive because you are fierce. My sister, continue to work on yourself to get better and stronger. You are not afraid of challenges or stepping up to the plate. I am so proud of you! I know where you have been and how far you have come in life. Do not let that fire in you burn out, nor let anyone take that from you. No one knows your story like you. At times we must take time out and reflect. This is only the beginning of remarkable things to come. Hard work does pay off! Keep striving and growing into the beautiful black butterfly that you are."

Love Your Big Sister,

Gigi

Fabulous: Unstoppable

How can a woman who has been through the fire, mud, and storms continue to push her way to be powerful and successful when staring hell in the face? She did not let the negativity disrupt what God had in store for her. No one knew that she was a single parent of three beautiful, energetic daughters. Her dedication to her children is the most important part of her life. She never wanted her children to live as if they were in a single-parent household or have the constraint of statistics of children being less likely to succeed because their mother walked away from an unconducive marriage to their father. She did not know how she would make it or provide for her children. She felt helpless! The struggle was real, and the embarrassment quickly set in when the lights were disconnected in her home. How can she face her children when she did not have the funds to turn the lights on? Her money was limited, and she was too prideful to ask for help. She was frantic because she did not know who would help her. Her children laughed at her because she had to get on food stamps to make sure there was food on the table for them. She had been a woman that had herself together. How could she be struggling like this? This was the lowest she had ever been in her life. The uncertainty of her being a good mother was the beginning of the catastrophe with the Department of Family & Children Services (DFACS).

The threats from DFACS were escalating, and it was becoming more apparent that her children would be displaced with their father. She worked tirelessly to provide the best she could for her family. If that meant she had to work two jobs and attend college as a full-time non-traditional student, then that is precisely what she did. Family meant the world to her. There was nothing she would not do for her family. No matter how many times they disagree, family will always be there for support. It was truly a blessing, and God sent her parents to be a resource to stand in the gap with her when it was difficult to provide for her children. Her parents absolutely loved their grandchildren and would give them the world. There were numerous times they would purchase school supplies and clothes every school term for her daughters. She cherished them for taking her children on several vacations a year to Florida when she did not have the means to do so. Her desires for her children stretched beyond the money and material things she could give them. The one thing she knew she could give her daughters was LOVE – a mother's love is priceless!

Somehow, DFACS and their manipulative father were indifferent. She hid the tears from her daughters as she cried at night because they did not know the pain she felt of losing them. The weight of the world was on her shoulders. The responsibilities as a parent come with many challenges to keep our children safe from society's unwanted terrors and craziness. When life shifted, and it was not always peaches and cream, she found ways to keep a smile on her children's faces. Yet, she lost the battle to remain with her children. She gave in and stopped fighting with the system to honor her children's wishes to live with their father. She was utterly heartbroken, and her world was upside down!

No one knew her story or the distress she endured over the years from losing guardianship of her daughters. She felt her daughters were resentful and frowned upon her because she was not living in an upscale neighborhood. Although her house on the south side of town was exceptionally clean, it did not meet the standards of their father's house on the north side of town in Buford, Georgia. The daughters she had raised for over 15 years as a single parent were now unfamiliar to her. She must get to know them all over again. So much has changed during the years of them living apart. However, something that did not change was the unconditional love she had for her babies. A mother wants nothing but the best for her children. She was happy they were doing well and growing up to be beautiful young women. Her daughters were going to a prominent school known for the best education in Gwinnett County. No matter how much she missed her daughters, she was proud of their accomplishments.

Even though it was extremely uncomfortable being apart from her children, she managed somehow to keep her faith. Meditation became a daily regimen to relax her mind from the failures she had to face. She wondered how God was going to turn her situation around. She asked God to see her through the pain and help her focus on her education. God revealed it to her. It was a whisper, and she heard it clearly, "The strength that got you through gang rape, abusive relationships, racism, strenuous college studies, and the lineage of strong, beautiful women in your family will be the driving force to push you to strive for excellence." God wants the absolute best for all his children. The power of the spirit can change the mindset to become more than a conqueror in any situation. During your lifetime, God will allow people to cross your path to help with his plan for success in your life.

The day she met Jeannie changed her life professionally and in business. The birth of her independent wine business (WineShop at Home) started from attending a wine tasting party at a friend's house. Jeannie was the wine consultant of that event. The light bulb went off instantly in her head that she needed to do business with Jeannie. She was eager to get more information about the wine business. Having her own business was always a short-term goal. Leaving a legacy for her children and grandchildren motivated her to work hard and hustle harder. Unfortunately, the motto of being replaceable in Corporate America is true. No matter how hard you work or how dedicated to your job you are, anyone is expendable. Her professional career as a Business Office Manager gave her gratification for over 30 years, but she needed more. Running her own business would create a path to freedom. Her Poppa taught her business and entrepreneurship all her life. He owned and managed several lucrative businesses around the Metro Atlanta Area and had not worked for anyone since 1988. He believed in her and raised her to be "ROYAL" since she was a little girl. She took heed to the long conversations regarding her independent freedom from a job and creating residual income for her children's future. Once the business platform was open to doing her thing, she jumped on board. Wine and conversation go together; it is indeed the perfect match.

She was always a huge fan of wine and knew she could be a successful wine consultant. Wine was second nature for her because she grew up with European customs. At 13 years old, her parents adopted European traditions to celebrate her teenage years by giving her the first glass of wine to drink. Let us just say she has been a wine lover ever since. Who would have thought the woman that had been through so much was still standing? She was not going to let her pain or traumas from her past determine her future. The thought of having her own business was far-fetched by some, but not by her. She wanted everything God promised her she could have. If she stayed true to herself and treated others kind, reaching for the stars would be easy by God's grace.

BLAST OFF!!! Her wine business took off like a rocket! She worked hard and kept working harder to change the game. This business afforded her the opportunity to collaborate with an influential team to coach her to be profitable in this endeavor. If she could handle money management in her profession as a Healthcare Business Office Manager, she knew her wine business would thrive as well. Being a Senior Wine Consultant for WineShop at Home has taken her business to the next level.

This has been a humbling experience because there is no "I "in the word team. Teamwork makes the dream work. Her dynamic team worked diligently to support the goals of the business. She had the pleasure to team up with an amazing mentor, Rochelle. Rochelle never hesitated to listen to the issues she was experiencing and always provided strategies to advance her wine business to a higher level. The critiques and responses from her wine tastings gave her the motivation she needed to elevate and become a better wine consultant. She had the opportunity to collaborate with other entrepreneurs on different events, such as Empowerment Gala's, Money & Mimosas, Wine & Wealth, Cigars & Wine Down Wednesdays, and Infinity Love Expos, to name a few.

Through her success in the wine business, she utilized her platform to start a cosmetic consulting business with Tori Belle Cosmetics. Her passion has always been the love of beauty, fashion, and hair. She loves people and knows beauty is far deeper than the surface. As an independent cosmetic consultant, being fabulous and unstoppable starts with the beautiful woman in the mirror. Although the woman in the mirror is attractive, she may not feel as attractive as she looks. Because of her passion for sisterhood, she wanted women to feel beautiful while having girl time or a girl's night out. Women tend to lose themselves in their families, careers, children, or just life. She knows this far too well because she had the same experience of losing herself. As a result, she wanted to unite both businesses to be a blessing for women to increase their self-esteem and beauty. The birth of Sipping Pretty, also known as Slay & Sip businesses, became an outlet for women to network, share ideas, and converse on life issues. It was an opportunity to cater to the woman within to be a beautiful reflection in the mirror. She did not want to change the woman but enhance her with beauty tips to boost self-confidence – what a wonderful way to bring women together and promote positive sisterhood. It was the perfect business decision to enjoy exquisite Artisan wines/champagnes and feel beautiful with Tori Belle cosmetics. We ALL are fabulous!

Free: Exhale

Finally, free to exhale from the past and move forward to the future. No one ever said it would be easy, but it would be worth the fight to succeed in life. When life kicked her down, she did not throw in the white towel; she pressed towards her purpose. She is a child of the Most High God. His anointing reigns through her and keeps her protected. She will not fail; she will only elevate in everything she does. If she keeps God first in all things, anything is possible. Today, she is free from abuse. It will no longer hinder her or destroy her character. She does not have to be afraid to love again and receive love. She can embrace her fears and open her heart to be loved as the beautiful queen she is. No longer will she run away from new experiences. She will change her mindset to overcome adversity, knowing she holds the keys to her success and the power to her future. Racism can not have her, and hatred will not destroy her faith.

Enemy, you have forgotten who her father God is! It is time to exhale, queen, because you're beautiful, smart, funny, charismatic, energetic, savvy, adventurous, happy, and full of life. Strength is behind your smile, so be you, be free to explore the world, be amazing, be creative. She can hold her head up high with dignity because she is an overcomer of trials and tribulations that could have driven her insane. God saved her so she could right her wrongs and be the woman He created her to be. Rape will not keep her bound. She is removing the shackles off her ankles and not looking back at the past. Her past made her as strong as she is today.

There's no more hiding in the shadow of her pain. She is a fighter and a sister soldier for her freedom. Exhale queen; you proved the naysayers wrong. She will decree and declare these things:

- Prosperity covers her children and her entire family abundantly.
- Unconditional love from her soulmate is waiting for her.
- She will not lack anything she needs.
- God will always provide for her.
- She does not look like what she has been through.
- Whatever she touches will turn to gold.
- Her businesses will be successful and lucrative.
- She will love her neighbor and be a support system to anyone that needs her.
- Motivation and encouragement will represent the woman, friend, sister, daughter, and mother she is.

Her motto is, "Life is too short to be anything but happy." Happy is all she wants to be in her life. She will uphold the slogan, "Live by choice, not by chance. Be motivated, not manipulated. Make changes, not excuses. Be useful, not used. Be selfless, not selfish. Excel in life, do not compete. Do something AMAZING." Meditation is good for the soul. The golden nuggets she lives by reflecting, revise, reconnect, regroup, and release. Do not hold on to baggage. Release the drama and negative influences that will keep you stagnated. Complacency is not an option for her. She wants the absolute best that life has to offer. She is a blessed woman, and her confidence will leave trails of glitter to inspire other women. Light will always follow her because darkness will not prevail.

By exposing her past, her wounds are bleeding. The hardened scabs of pain and rejection have been removed to start the healing process. Her trust in God will illuminate her journey for greatness. She will shine bright like a diamond. Isaiah 53:5, "But he was wounded for our transgressions, he was bruised for our iniquities: the chastisement of our peace was upon him; with his stripes, we are healed," will be upon her life. All her sins are forgiven. She will be healed from broken heartedness. She is finally at peace with a promising life ahead. This is the story of my life. I am her. She is me. Shame is no longer the woman I am. I have been set free.

This is my truth. It is my time to exhale! Shine, shine, beautiful sister, shine and get your blessings!

3.

Biography

Keisha "ShonGee" Grant is the CEO and Founder of ShonGee Enterprises, LLC, Co-Author of "I Am A Woman Empowered: Fierce, Fabulous, & Free Anthology Volume II," Senior Independent Wine Consultant for A Wine Shop at Home, and an Independent Cosmetics Consultant for Tori Belle Cosmetics. Keisha is the proud mother of three beautiful girls that keep her going and motivate her to succeed in life. Keisha's eagerness to learn and apply educational principles positioned her in her professional career of 30 years as a healthcare professional. She attended Clayton State University and achieved her undergraduate degree in Healthcare Management in 2019.

Keisha utilized her platforms to collaborate with other business-minded entrepreneurs for business expos, vendor services, women conferences, and marketing objectives by introducing her business to the community. Keisha has a passion for people and enjoys sharing positive vibes along her journey of success. Her creative soul and energetic spirit loves to inspire women by uplifting their self-esteem to adore the woman reflected in the mirror. Keisha's enthusiasm for fashion, beauty enhancers, variety of hair styles/hair products inspired her to expand her platform to the cosmetic industry to launch her business "Sipping Pretty," also known as "Slay & Sip." Sipping Pretty is inspired to be an outlet for women to network, be themselves, and converse with other beautiful women making boss moves in life and in their careers. Keisha desires to be an activist in the community as a mentor and the voice behind teenage girls in domestic violence, victims of sexual abuse, and confidence strengthening.

II

Chef LaToya Larkin

4.

Dedication

As we know being a woman, we wear many hats in the midst of living this thing called life. This story is righteously dedicated to all the single mothers holding it down and especially those raising boys on their own. Yes, sis, I'm talking to you. The one balancing kids, work, the household, putting yourself through school, and running that side business that is on the brink of becoming a full-time gig. All while trying to stay afloat and not lose her mind. Sister Queen, you are one of a kind financing your household one hundred percent in full on the strength of morals, ambition, and drive, backed with a vision of excellence for themselves and their children.

Can I shout out the hopeless romantic lover? The one who has a beautiful spirit, mind, and heart and simply wants to be loved in this day and age of dating. Yet, find herself being misunderstood and can't get it right in the wonderful world of love. Or the woman that is caught up in that toxic relationship that you know you should have left years ago, but so in love and has so much vested. They just don't have the strength to walk away and find themselves in the cycle of toxicity trying to do the right thing with the wrong person.

We can't forget my favorite. The one who has been through all the above listed and now realizes, wait a minute, they got me f****d up. Yeah, I've been through it and can be real with myself and face my truth as I lost myself over the years. I now know what things are truly hitting for. You can no longer hold me to those standards and ways of my past. Those days are RIP dead and gone because I am now Fierce, Fabulous, and Free.

Last, I couldn't leave out my solid ride or die. Without this young man, I wouldn't be where I am, Xaviar Carmello Whatley, you are my reason and my WHY. They say if your WHY doesn't make you cry, then it's not big enough. Anytime I think of not being able to provide for you or putting your well-being at stake, it will always bring me to my knees and remind me how and why I do what I do.

5.

I Earned My Glow-Up Degree from Net Worth University Chef LaToya Larkin, MBA, CCE

What Does It Mean to be Fierce, Fabulous, and Free

At the ripe age of 40, I can confidentially and proudly say that I am fierce, fabulous, and truly free. I have gotten to this point in my life because I did the work. Trust and believe the journey was difficult, and it has not always been that way, regardless of how it may have looked on the outside looking in. I'm talking about a point where I know exactly who LaToya Cherie Larkin (government name) is. However, you may know me professionally as Chef Larkin, Chef LaToya, or Chefdivah. My close friends know me as Toya or Nook. On a side note, if you know me by Nook, then we really go way back because only people I grew up with call me Nook. However, you may know me, take the pick.

No, seriously, I know what I am tolerating. I know my level of flexibility to compromise and what I will bend and fold on. I am ok with someone who has my best interest calling me to the carpet on questionable moves. I do so while proudly holding my head high and holding myself accountable for any shortcomings my circle sees fit. I treat people respectfully and fairly, with a high level of regard for people's time, resources, and efforts. Why is that? Simple, I learned the importance of healthy boundaries, mindset, and accountability – which all are key components to being fierce, fabulous, and free.

Qualities of a Triple Threat

Have you ever seen a woman that intentionally moves in her purpose? It seems like everything she touches turns to gold. Every shot she calls for herself somehow manifests itself. Every time you turn around, she's being honored and awarded. It appears she has this magnetic, charismatic charm about her that lights up the room when she walks in and engages with total strangers and even those of whom she knows. She does everything with grace, poise, elegance, and class. Yet operates on a wish creed, wishing someone would check her because she could not care less what anyone would have to say about what she does or how she does it. I'm talking about sis is the one that is getting things done so unapologetically and giving the haters a performance of a lifetime. When all they can do is give a standing ovation as bad as they don't want to give it to her. If you have seen this woman, or even perhaps you are this woman. Then, my Sister Queen, I'm here to tell you-you are indeed a solidified triple threat of the 3 F's: "Fierce, Fabulous, and Free."

However, it takes time and awakening to get to that point – a point where you experience an awakening in your life that shakes your core like an earthquake and whirlwind your soul like a category 5 hurricane. Something of such magnitude then you must really go thru the trials and tribulations that will forever shift your outlook on life and your perspective of realities and transform your mindset on how you once processed and handled situations, which will level you up to live that life of abundance that God has planned for you. Part of that comes with learning how to confront painful past traumas and take adequate time to heal. The things you used to find pleasure and comfort in doing have come to where you have outgrown those habits you are no longer doing. I know I'm talking to somebody that was the once upon a time librarian. You know, the one that lived for a good read then sip their tea overlooking the teacups brim. I mean the one that would read you like a book. Come up one side and drop on the other side, then whip around front to back to go along with that side-to-side action. Though now things are different when someone tries you. Instead of giving that tit for tat energy as you once oozed. All you can do is just simply smile and say something positive because you now know that when people go for the jugular, they are clearly miserable with their lives and hurting on the inside. Then, not to mention our lovely former FLOTUS Michelle Obama taught us to go high when the haters go low. Growth has resulted because you have been stretched like a rubber band yet never snapped. Now let's not get it twisted. There have been many times and days that you thought you would do just that, but your resilience kept you intact. You have literally put in the grind and did all the holistic self-work. You attended the school of hard knocks, aka Net Worth University, putting in the blood, sweat, and tears to get your Glow Up Degree that now allows you to be Fierce, Fabulous, and Free.

The Three F's

Now let's put each word under the scope. When I think of "Fierce," I think of something or someone fearless, extremely passionate, diligent, intentional, purposeful, unstoppable, with unrestrained zeal, and RHOlentless, aka relentless. You may wonder, wait, RHOlentless, what does it mean to be RHOlentless? I know what relentless is, but not sure that I have heard of RHOlentless. Don't worry; I will share the meaning behind it shortly. Keep in mind, though, a relentless grind will shift your dreams into a reality.

Then let's look at "Fabulous" without an unwavering doubt. Fabulous is something that is extraordinary, exceptional, phenomenal, unheard of, and amazing. Today's black women are living fabulously and fiercely beyond their ancestors' wildest dreams. Doing things that our great grandparents could never do or thought they could do.

Last, "Free" is just what it is and almost a no-brainer that comes to mind of not being under the control of or in the power of another and doing what you want to do when you want to do things with no limits or restraints. Notice how each wordplay on each other, and when all put together, it gives unapologetic warm & fuzzy vibes. You know those powerful vibrations of energy that you feel and recognize when you see someone admirable and think to yourself. Oh yeah, sis is walking and serving in her purpose doing the damn thang. As the popular saying goes, "she understands the assignment."

Healthy Boundaries

Healthy Boundaries are essential and critical to your self-development and growth as a person. It plays a crucial component in the three Fs. Without those needed healthy boundaries, it can weigh heavily on you like a ton of bricks and become mentally exhausting. I've learned many lessons in life on this earth in 40 years, and one big takeaway is with people. They only do what you allow them to do, and if allowed, people will put you on a leash and walk you like a dog. Sit tight. I will speak about my 6-year dog walk later. Sadly, in life, some people are conditioned to give others the leash and will forever stay on the leash and allow them to treat them however the other person feels fit because their low self-esteem and insecurities enable that type of treatment. Establishing those healthy boundaries is the requisite as you walk in the pathway of the fierce, fabulous, and free journey.

Mindset is Everything

Mindset is a central working piece of the puzzle in this journey called life. The way a person processes and handles a situation speaks volumes about their mindset. I've experienced many situations that revolved around the mindset and thinking about how someone could process and even get that out of the situation at hand. Let me share a mindset story. Back when I taught, I was that teacher that fellow educators to the administrators and, of course, the parents and kids loved. Many times, when I saw my coworkers in passing, they would always have something positive to say, recognizing the work that is being done with my chefs. Then when I met the parents, I would get the looks and always hear. "Oh, you are Chef Larkin, that's all we hear about at the house Chef Larkin, this Chef Larkin that, today Chef said. It's finally good to put a name with a face." It was always a good feeling because it made me feel I am divinely serving in my purpose and loving on my students the way they needed to be loved, not to mention I was being impactful and teaching the lessons required. Let's be honest, who is receptive to learning from someone they can't stand, have no respect, or regard for? Most parents, especially the dads, always commented with a warm smile, leaving that fuzzy feeling.

Then, sadly, a few parents over the years weren't so warm and cozy. They were colder like iced tea, and it was always the mothers and my fellow sisters that looked like me that would smile in my face, but I could see the resistance and that look of hate in their eyes, which was always disheartening because I always treated my students as my own. I always thought and operated in a mama auntie mode. I was old enough to be my student's mother and have been an auntie since I was eleven years old. I know it was always a good feeling to have teachers who care and will go the extra mile for my son when I am not around being a part of my village. So, I tried to always be that to my parents and that extra extension of help to keep their children on the right track.

I will leave this memorable parent anonymous, but when I met her, she was so nice. She skinned and grinned in my face as if she liked me. She even befriended me on social media, showed so much fake love with comments and reactions, and stayed in my DM. I know the problem deep down that resonated in her was the fact that her child admired and looked up to me in a way that he would never view his own mother. Not to mention we had a dope cut straight from the brick type relationship as I had with most of my students, but this particular student, we were very close. A year after he graduated, a classmate passed away from a tragic car accident. He made a post on social media about the passing, and I made a comment when I realized who the student was.

The mother came for me out of nowhere, saying that I was self-righteous and didn't say sorry for your loss. Yet, I gave my condolences and partnered with a group of teachers to do something for the family that she had no clue about. She then took it further and jumped in the DM to go in for the kill, calling me all kinds of b*****s and h**s. I'm talking about literally trying to tear me down to make herself feel and look good. I have no life and nothing going for myself, though I have two businesses and completing two others in my culinary collective. I'm stupid with a degree, yet I have two degrees and working on number three. I can't cook, and she can out cook me, but people pay me to cook for them, and no one pays her to cook for them. My students hate me, and no one likes me, yet during Christmas time, I'm the one teacher leaving on the holiday break with a cart to load up gifts to my car from all my students who hate me. Or when I tell students things going on in other classes, they are ready to come and check the other class. She'll pull up on me and will spit in my face when she sees me because I'm a scary bougie b***h. Not knowing I'm a former recovering, you got me f****d up fixer slash breaker upper. You know, the Petty Patty's in life that live to fix someone and break them up, as the old folks used to say, with a lesson that will stick for life. Or how I grew up and spent some time in the streets when I was younger and still associated with people I grew up and ran with who are still about that life with NOTHING to lose – the ones who know where the dead bodies are at, yeah, them boys. One better she didn't know, I have a concealed handgun license with a registered gun and will bust a cap first and ask questions later if my safety and well-being is on the line because Texas is that type of state. Again, not knowing I'm cut from that cloth no matter how bougie and stuck up I may appear to be. I know you are probably thinking, is this real? I swear I couldn't make this up if I tried, and to think all of that stemmed from me saying, "I'm sorry to hear that and will uplift her family, friends, and classmates in prayers" and did not say "sorry for your loss ." Mind you, there is more than one way to express condolences, but since I didn't say verbatim, "sorry for your loss." That was the justification to tell me about myself since, in her mind, I was not me giving my condolences. Know that the old me would have lit her up like a firecracker and been ready to pull up for the action. However, my elevated position in business, building my brand, and being a leader in the community couldn't allow me to stoop to that level.

Though the heavenly father himself came down and put the squeeze on your girl to wrap me tight on that day, I saw the certified construction worksite of red flags, orange cones, yellow tape, white markings, and lime green vest a long time ago of who she was and what she was about. However, I played it cool to see how long it would take to expose her hand with me because amid her buttering up to me. She would talk her nieces and other family business to me, looking for a reaction, but I never dignified the comments with a response or entertained it because it showed me that no matter how cool you claim to be with me. You had the ill intent in your heart and mind from the misery of her life. Seriously, she exposed her nieces and their mother by airing out their family business that I already knew from the nieces confiding in me because they were my former students as well. However, what if I didn't know what you spoke about?

You just dropped all their business at my doorstep because you were in your feelings mad at them during the moment. How can one be fierce, fabulous, and free? Living a tit for tat life, staying ready to fix and one up a person when someone wrongs me by doing and saying mean nasty things to me. It's not possible positivity can't exist where negativity lives.

The Birth of RHOlentless

Let me share a quick story of how RHOlentless came to be. Picture this 2013, a promising new year of many great new starts. In January, I had started grad school at Springfield College in Organizational Management and Leadership and online to pledge with the Illustrious Sigma Gamma Rho Sorority, Inc. I had moved into a new apartment that had the perfect layout and couldn't wait for the warmer weather in the spring and summer to host events and decorate the large oversized balcony that led out of my bedroom and living room area. In February, I had just quit my job of being a District Chef Trainer that required extensive travel around the beautiful, great state of Texas for the past 2.5 years and started with the Houston Food Bank working with the Texas Department of Criminal Justice (TDCJ) Inmates and Harris County Probationers coordinating the Serving for Success program as a Culinary Instructor. I was super excited about all the newness to come to enjoy the fruits of my labor and felt like this was it. Great job, amazing new place, and becoming Greek while obtaining my MBA. You could not have told me that life was not good.

March 4, 2013, my life changed drastically in a way that I would never have imagined. It was my first day of work, and I was so sick from the weekend of having a nasty cold. All I could think of on my first day at my new job at the Houston Food Bank during orientation was how I couldn't wait to go home, take a shower, meds, and get in my comfy bed after a long day. I left work in a hurry, ready for rest and relaxation. Turning down the street, I saw every first responder there was in the community, fire department, police department, and ambulances. I thought to myself, dang, that's messed up. It looks like it was a fire.

My balcony is the perfect spot to be nosey and post up to check out the scene when I get settled in the house. When I finally got to my apartment building, I started thinking, wait, that looks like my building. Man, I hope my place is intact because lord knows my body is tired and achy. I'm ridiculously hoarse, and my throat is so dry and sore. I just need rest. I got out of my car and walked up, and the normal walkway area was blocked off. So, I stopped a neighbor and asked, "Hey, what building was on fire." She was replied, "Oh baby, it's building one." My heart started racing, and I nervously replied, "wait, which apartment units because I live in building one. She asked which apartment, I replied "112". She looked at me with such pain and compassion in her eyes and said, "baby, I'm so sorry, but you don't have nothing. The fire started in the unit right next to you, and it spread so fast that it destroyed the unit it started in and the other units in proximity. The windy conditions did not make any better." In a total state of shock, it felt like someone knocked the wind out of me, and the next thing I knew, the tears started rolling down my face. I felt the lump in my throat, but no sound would come out because I was so hoarse and sick from the cold I had contracted over the weekend. I was with nothing minus what I left home for work this morning, in a matter of a day. I started out with everything I wanted, needed, plus more, all to come home only to own the possession of the clothes on my back, shoes on my feet, and purse on my shoulder. I was devastated. Everything I worked so hard for, all our (my son and I) belongings, were up in smoke, literally.

Not to mention we lost our pet Twinkles. She was a beautiful Siamese cat with a tan body, chocolate ears, tail, and paws, with icy blue eyes that twinkled. I hated cats but loved that cat. She was so laid back and wasn't catty like most cats are. I know you're thinking not catty like cats, but she's a cat. What other way would she be? I mean that because she didn't scratch furniture or jump on prominent fixtures. Probably the highest she would jump would be on the back of the couch and onto my bed to lie on my back. I grew up a dog person, but as I got older loved the self-sufficiency in cats, and again, she was chill and laid back like a dog. I then got on the phone and called my family to tell them what had happened. Of course, I was in distress and couldn't figure out why this had to happen to me at this moment. I had done everything right. Finally felt like everything was falling into place, and now this. My mama kept saying, "don't worry, all those things are materialistic and can be replaced. Besides, you have State Farm, and that's the best insurance. You will be just fine. If you need me to send you money until I get back in town, then I'll send you money, but just be grateful that you and that baby were not at home. God is about to bless you with better". Of course, she was right. It was so devastating because 100 units were destroyed, and only three people had renters' insurance. Luckily, I had the mindset to invest in renters' insurance because of the job I had when I traveled. I was gone so much I was afraid someone would break into my townhome while I was gone. So, I purchased a policy, and let me be the one to say that it was the best $20 p/month spent to get a $30K payout to start over. Later that evening, I was thinking as I listened to Alicia Keys, Brand New Me, at my new residence of the Holiday Inn for the next month that my insurance put me at until I found a new place. I called my line sisters and big sister to let them know what happened, along with a few other people. In less than 72 hours, I received an overwhelming response of donated clothes and toiletries for my son and me. Then, over the next few days and weeks, monetary donations started flooding my mother's mailbox from all over the state. My people from my old job at my designated accounts sent money for my son and me to get back on track.

I was set to cross the burning sands and become a Soror of Sigma Gamma Rho Sorority, Inc. in six days on March 9, 2013. At my crossing, I was given the name RHOlentless. As they explained, you are so strong and fearless. You picked yourself back up in less than a week with everything that happened. Most people would have crumbled and fallen apart, but besides this, just your energy and spirit, everything about you is RHOlentless. A few lessons learned from that experience of the many to come on the fierce, fabulous, and free journey – one was that total strangers and people I've known in a short time came to my aid versus the tenured people I've known for a lifetime.

Tax Season and Self Worth Valuation

The biggest disappointment was that with everything going on and all the people who were there for me, the one person who I thought would be there for me was not there for me. Turned his cheek because, minus all the things I tried to do to show him my growth, he still held me the standards and regards to how I used to be when I was younger and selfish. You may wonder what standards and regards I was being held to. When I was younger, I always maintained and dealt with older men who catered to me and spoiled me. In the heat of the moment, he would say mean things like I used my body to get what I want and constantly reminded me he's not a trick. He was so bent on keeping one up that it appeared he was always trying to tear me down to build himself up. I always felt some low-key resentment because he would say things like how you do just live the way you do. You live such a great life. In my mind, it's like, ugh, let down your guard and come live with me. Let's just be carefree, love each other, and live life, but it was much more complex than that for him. He was also jaded from the bitter dealings of the ex-wife racking him over the coals in uneconomical child support. So, he always made it clear and no secret his kids come first, and he's not tricking. This really stung because I thought this person was my one, and all I wanted was a life with him. We grew up together as childhood friends, high school and college sweethearts that grew apart, but I just knew that divine intervention to bring us back together for a reason. That it did, however, not for what I thought. Despite all the mental anguish I put up with, I loved this man unconditionally. I put a death grip on tenured familiarity and sadly got stuck holding onto the loving, kind young man I once knew. As Maya Angelou said, when someone shows you who they are, believe them. I had every signal and sign show up on my Doppler radar but just couldn't accept the realities of the man that was presented before me. I lost myself in loving this person because I was in love with an illusion of someone that would never see me how I saw him or treat me the way I treated him nor love me how I loved him. He was so hurt and broken from the previous two failed marriages before that transpired from our time apart upon us reconnecting at 29. He wasn't the best man to a woman, but a wonderful father and excellent provider who pays bills. On paper, he was ideal HBCU educated, Greek & Mason affiliated, great paying job, almost six figures, and charming to women because he was a man that loved his mother. All those outstanding qualities plus the tenure always kept me around, but I realized none of that makes any difference because when someone has a certain perspective of you. You could find a cure for their sick parent's cancer and if they still choose to hold on to the negative associated with you. Then you have put in all the work for nothing.

There was love between us without a doubt, but it was so toxic. I'm talking about that toxic narcissistic type of love. I was breaking my own heart because the harsh reality was that he would never look at me as anything other than someone to share intimate moments, as he liked to put it kindly. We'd make plans, and he would stand me up with no regard, like time didn't matter and that I just needed to get over the fact that there was a last-minute change of plans if he called that shot. Then when I called him on it, he would get mad and try to flip the script like I didn't have a right to be upset and I was overreacting, but would never stand me up to pull up late at night. My head was so far up his ass in hopes the blinders would soon come off, and he would choose me, but neither ever happened. I always thought, "why not me. If you just gave me a chance, then I would properly love you the way you never been loved". That is what I always told myself.

The mind-altering experience came when I found out he was sleeping with someone I knew, and one day after work, I received a phone call from her and another woman he was sleeping with who thought she was pregnant, and they were in a relationship. It was a petty attempt to let me know he was getting around and a messy attempt to bust him and bring all his dirt to the surface. As I reflect and look back, my self-esteem was so low and shot because I was literally going so far out of my way trying to show him who I was. I remember one time I drove 6.5 hours back to Houston and cooked a gourmet Asian spread. All for him to come over just to have dinner and leave to hang out with friends, as he says. Though for all I know could have been another woman. I didn't want to say anything because I was trying to keep the peace, as I know he was going through a lot to heal from all the hurt and trauma. I was so hurt because I was really looking forward to spending the entire evening with him as I enjoyed the time spent when things were cool and had no drama. I thought I would be regarded for my travel time and cooking everything from scratch. I was just so glad to spend whatever time we could because I was also trying to give him space to heal and not press any issues too far. Regardless of what was done, nothing seemed to be enough to be chosen. I prided myself on the fact that he could not leave me alone and that whenever I called him, he would come. It's crazy looking back because he would always commit to a night of intimacy but would never commit to a relationship. Then again, who would leave someone alone when they know they can have access to someone at any given time and that the person is wrapped around their finger.

That right there is when it hit me; Sis, wake the f**k up. You have already spent most of your 30s stressed, depressed, and in love with someone who will never return what you give. He gave you that bs about not wanting a relationship, yet he started a relationship with another woman. Who had lost a baby and thought she was pregnant again? You deserve so much more. Yeah, you're in your 30s and thought you would be married by now because you love "love" and see everyone around you married or in relationships, but it's time to get busy doing you, and that's exactly what I did. 2016, I finally gained the gumption to put a plan in motion and boss up. I had weight loss surgery and resolved my diabetes by taking the reins back on my health. I maintained my weight by incorporating meal preps into my personal chef service business. This way, I made money and was forced to eat right at the same time because I would meal prep food for myself on the back end of my paid clients. I started building up my personal credit and taking my business concepts more seriously. I always had plans not to be the 30–40-year teacher. Now is the time to make it happen and execute my years and years of thought-out plans that I had been working on since the recession in 2008.

I realized exactly who I was and what it was hitting for with me after six years of a plethora of lessons learned. I then went back to school and got my MBA. While in grad school, I started working on Its Thyme 4 a Change (501 c3) on the schoolwork. So, when I graduated, I had a fully planned nonprofit. Along with that, I launched my million-dollar baby Black Girl Tamales and Divah Chef Apparel to complete my culinary collective. Funny thing, now I laugh at how crazy I was in love with someone that wouldn't even take me on a trip or have any fun positive moments. Oh yeah, travel has become a favorite pastime. I now only deal with men who will appreciate the things I bring to the table and cater to me, but catering to me, and I do not use them. Because I'm blessed to be at a point in life where I can finance myself and don't need another man for his money and what he can do for me, spoiling me with riches. I had to retire the acrobatic circus act of jumping through flaming hoops, walking on stilts, and trying to tame the tiger by showing and proving to someone like I once did to see me for me. From 2021 and beyond, Chef LaToya Larkin is Fierce, Fabulous, and Free.

6.

Biography

Chef LaToya Larkin is a transformational, life visionary strategist, impactful speaker, and co-author of Woman Empowered: Fierce, Fabulous, and Free, an anthology that empowers women to live limitless lives, celebrates confidence and discovers true self-worth. But once you are in her presence, it doesn't take long to realize that she is a woman of impact and knows no bounds. She is a divah. She is rholentless. An unleasher. A ceiling shatterer who proves that when powered by passion, focus, and drive, women are unstoppable.

Known for her culinary flare, intelligence, effortless sophistication, style, and grace, Chef Larkin is a woman who instantly shifts every space she steps into. In her highly successful restaurant and education career, what she found she loved most was introducing people, particularly women, to upgrade mindsets and empowering them to develop into someone beyond their wildest dreams.

Yet, behind the scenes of her own picture-perfect image, few knew that Chef LaToya experienced many setbacks and failures that created much self-doubt and insecurities in her journey. However, she was determined to fight her way through. She felt a stirring in her soul for a larger life, so she followed her first love of the hustle and cooking to see where it would lead. After 12 years of hard work, dedication, the Pandemic, and a dream-defining interview plus a written article by Cuisine Noir, bought her into the homes and on the radars of foodies across the country, she knew she was where she belonged and created something of a powerful magnitude. Full of fresh purpose, Chef Larkin walked away from her guaranteed, government contract checks of being a public-school educator to freelance all concepts full time.

Fueled to find ways to next-level women's mindsets and lives, Chef LaToya has launched mentorship and consulting class sessions, besides her thriving preexisting concepts: Black Girl Tamales creative fusion tamales, Its Thyme 4a Change 501 c3 nonprofit, clothing line Divah Chef Apparel of shirts and aprons to awaken the possibility of more. Transcending the culinary visionary industry, Chef Larkin's businesses and brand have morphed into a mission, stylishly signing permission slips of women who had forgotten who they were.

Having never met a "no" that she will accept, Chef LaToya exemplifies an inner courage that is undeniably contagious. Whether she is in front of an audience of one or one hundred, with every word, she reminds women what they can do, be and have. With a practical, yet incredibly powerful formula of awakening, action, and acceleration, she guides women through the radical transformation required to shift their respective mindsets.

Chef Larkin is here for all women, ranging from young adolescent ladies to our seasoned cultured pearls from all walks of life. Specifically, the woman who needs to break out of the box of doubt, disappointment, and disbelief. She is here for the woman who needs to stop believing the bold lies she's been told about herself. She is here for the woman who needs to reimagine who and what she can be and unleash the Divah woman within.

III

Jasmine D. Milhouse

7.

Dedication

I dedicate this chapter to everyone that has made an impact in my life. Good, bad, and ugly, it made me the woman that I am.

For that, I am grateful.

8.

Guess What, Sis? You Win!

Sissss!!! Do you know that you have been through so much in your life? I hope you caught the key part in that question…BEEN THROUGH. That means every situation that has transpired in your life, you have conquered and pushed through it. I know this from experience. Now, I will not bore you with every inch and cranny of my life, but there are some key areas that I will speak on that will help me drive my points home for you. Take a walk with me if you will. Picture Louisiana, June 12, 1985, here comes me hollering as I enter this thing called life. We all come here not knowing anything about ourselves. As time passes and things happen, you begin to learn a lot about yourself, but sometimes we bury the good stuff and wear the bad stuff like a badge of honor. Let me explain.

Instead of walking in triumph, we walk in trials. There are moments when we get more satisfaction in knowing we are in the valley versus celebrating when we make it out. The key is to know how to celebrate not only when you come out but also while you are in there. Life becomes sweeter when you can stand up or sit down proudly with who you are. This was not so easy for me growing up. I am a sexual abuse survivor, and it all happened between the ages of 5 and 15. You can only imagine how much hell I mentally went through those ten years, physically too, might I add. I will spare you the details because I already wrote about those.

My journey into adulthood was one of the scariest things ever. I became a mother at the age of 16 as a result of being fast and getting sweet nothings whispered in my ear. Then BOOM, here comes my brown-eyed baby girl. At the young age of 16, I was kicked out of the church because I became pregnant with my daughter. I would have gladly taken any "disappointment" conversations, but the door was slammed in my face, and I was not allowed to come back. After I had my daughter, I went back to the people and asked for their forgiveness so that I could be a part of the church again, but I never asked God for His forgiveness, nor did I forgive myself. Being young and immature, I became angry that God would allow them to treat me in such a way, for I was only 16. How many of you know that I became angry with the wrong one? Who was I to teach her what it is like to become a woman when I was still a little girl myself?

Situations come with our choices, and we often don't make the best decisions. Guess what? Sometimes that is just the way life goes. Everything is not going to go the way we want it to go, but that is when you must empower yourself through those journeys. Sitting in a dark room rocking is ok, but it is not ok to stay there. Empowerment is like encouragement; it is good to get it from other sources, but you must develop the mental muscle to give it to yourself. I remember a very old song that says, "I'm somewhere down in the valley trying to get home." That is so true for many of us. When we are going through, we are searching in the dark for our way back out to the light, and we don't know how to push forward. Let me give you a smidge of insight on how you can start with some baby steps of empowerment.

1. Start a morning routine of praise and prayer – Rolling over and grabbing your phone is no longer an option going forward. Spending time with yourself and God is one of the best things you can ever do to begin your morning. The foundational start of your day can determine how you handle different situations throughout the day—not giving honor where it is due causes you not to

honor yourself as well. You have to set the tone of what you will respond to for the rest of the day.

2. Practice a self-care routine – Don't take this the wrong way, but that also includes washing your face, body, hair, and brushing your teeth. People can get so far from themselves that they lose the sense of the basics, such as those mentioned. Trust me; if you have not reached this point, you are doing better than you think. Treat yourself to a spa day, therapy session, or even a manicure/pedicure.

3. Clean up your house – Yes, this includes your house physically and spiritually. Sometimes we allow ourselves to get in such a funk that we neglect our residential home as well as our physical and spiritual home. Take a good look at yourself and your surroundings and examine who or what is beneficial and necessary. It is time to cut the cord to the things that are causing you the most negative side effects. It clears so much cloudiness and boosts your confidence.

4. Trust yourself to get the job done – When you believe in yourself, it changes your perspective on so many situations. Does that mean fear won't rise? No, that isn't what that means; however, it will cause you to change your verbiage and thought process when setting goals and tackling them head-on. Before you put your feet on the floor, you should be giving thanks to God for creating such an incredible person like you. Express heartfelt gratitude that you don't look like what you've been through. Smile at the things that were meant to kill you but made you stronger.

If I can be completely honest, there are days that I must coach myself to keep putting one foot before the other. I am not here to make it seem as if I have it all together because I know I don't.

Life is not about having it all figured out; it is about how to take what you've been through and discover the fierce, fabulous, and free side that has been inside of you all along. There is a yearning that is reaching out for the better side of life, and I knew that I had to reach back for it. I found myself at a point in life where nothing made sense. I was more of a people pleaser and made sure that everyone else was good while neglecting myself. Thinking about me was just unheard of because I mean, who was I? I had to make sure my family was good, the job was good, and my friends were good. I was drowning in a sea of people and never made sure I was able to swim. Crazy right? There's nothing new under the sun, but here I felt like I was Superwoman, and couldn't nobody survive unless I made sure they were good. TUH, honey, was I mistaken. In the midst of helping others, I lost sense of what I was responsible for. It caused my house to lack, and I was not the best mom that I could be.

Going to work and coming home like I was on autopilot became my life. Having fun with my children was not even on my radar. Knowing my worth? Forget about it! I had reached a point in life where I was either rescuing others, being heartbroken, or being taken advantage of. I was of no use to anyone, not even myself—still trying to be there for everybody while also teaching women how to be there for themselves. I had to take a step back. I became mentally drained because I was not pouring all that I was giving back into myself. I was not living what I was preaching, and it felt like I was going towards a brick wall at high speed with no brake line in sight.

God would show me visuals of who He wanted me to be, and I became terrified of myself. Wanting to be liked and accepted, I would dumb down around certain people because I didn't want anyone to think I felt like I was all that or knew it all. In all actuality, I was acting like a punk. I had absolutely no confidence in myself. Dressing up was a bare minimum, and when I did, it was not anything flattering, nor did I feel like I looked good in anything. There are only so many compliments you can receive from others, but nothing is like giving them to yourself.

Understanding the power of my words was not something I knew about. Again, I was in survival mode: work, pay bills and take care of my children. Instilling confidence in my children was natural, but it somehow didn't come through that well for me. I could not figure out what was going wrong. It was only when I started counseling sessions that I discovered I was the people person and the yes girl. I was always there for everybody but not there for myself. I looked for validation and acceptance in everything I did because I didn't feel like I was good enough.

We are all born with an inner purpose, but we must go through life to discover bits and pieces of it until reality hits one day. You will not fully understand your true purpose until you get free from things happening around you and people trying to control you. For the life of me, I could not figure out why I was always the provider for everyone. I wanted to make sure people had what they needed to survive. I was more concerned for them than they were themselves. One day God took everything away from me that would allow me to be there for people. I was jobless, carless, and homeless. I lost everything in a matter of two weeks. When in a situation like that, you do not have a choice but to find out how resilient you really are. Within 30 days, I was working again, bought another car, and had a place to stay.

I had to be there for me because no one else had the capability to provide what I needed. That is in no way to shame them because it is not for anyone to provide, be there, or take care of me. I had to encourage and empower myself daily with positive words. Speaking what I saw until I saw what I said became real for me. Wanting better is one thing, but knowing you deserve better is a whole different mindset. That is where I had to go because I knew for a fact less than was not in God's plan. We often quote scripture in such a cliché way, not knowing that it is meant to build your natural state to match your spiritual state. Baby, once I recognized that I had the ability to speak life into me, it was look out world because here she is. Not here I come because I was already here.

We sometimes must catch up to who we were created to be, and that is all I had to do. Being catapulted into self-love was just what I needed. Often, we gravitate towards the things we really need in our lives and think we can teach others when in actuality, we are learning more about ourselves as well. Learning about me and applying daily principles of self-love was like peeling back onion layers because I had to get to the core of me and work on her. Having the principles and strategies to apply in my life brought me to an important realization...I am whole by myself, and everything and everyone else is a bonus.

It took me away from being a people pleaser when I understood that I was created and born whole. I started taking myself on dates alone and having the time of my life. Was it a scary thing at first? Absolutely. Imagine going to a bar or nice restaurant and getting a table for one to eat a good meal alone...it sounds good even typing it now. However, when I first started doing it, I felt like a fish out of water. I would turn off my ringer and just sit to enjoy a glass of wine or a nice fancy drink, order an appetizer, a meal, and depending on the night, even a dessert. Baby, I had to get to me before I could show anybody anything. This has been an amazing uphill/downhill journey, and I wouldn't take anything for my journey now. Why not? Well, I am glad you asked. Had I chosen another route or regretted anything, I would not be who I am today. I would be in an identity crisis, trying to figure out who I am because I would have been too busy trying to be someone else. After getting to know me, I realized that I am a force to be reckoned with.

1. Sexual abuse – survived
2. Physical abuse – survived

3. Bullying – survived
4. Voiceless – speaking on international platforms
5. Homeless – sheltered
6. Suicidal thoughts – survived

That is just to name a few. When I look back over my life and all that I have come through, it brings tears to my eyes because I am still here. It goes back to the beginning. I got through it, and now I can share my story with so many people. So, am I fierce, fabulous, and free? You bet your life I am because I have earned everything God has in store for me. Are there days when I must push myself still? Yes, because we never get to the point where we have arrived. There is a test that we must get through at every level, and it keeps us growing more and more. When you stop growing, you die.

In closing of my little Easter speech, if you didn't take anything from what all I have said, let me sum it up again. There was once a little girl who went through some of the most trying times that a child should not have to go through. It made her bitter, angry, and full of hatred. That little girl became a promiscuous teenager, which led her to get pregnant at an immature age—thrown into adulthood while still being a child herself. That same little girl developed into Superwoman, whose kryptonite was herself. She was her own weakness because her actions towards herself pulled from her strength. That young woman was underdeveloped mentally, spiritually, and emotionally. One day that young woman woke up a full-grown woman and came to the realization that she did not need validation and acceptance from people because God had already instilled her with permission and access to be who she was called to be. Everything and everyone were just a benefit, and whoever was not, she had the option to deal or let go.

Be free in your decisions and go within to find your freedom. It is a great feeling over here. Again, understand that you won't just wake up, and all will be a gravy train. That is the beautiful part for me because, at every level, I discover a new area of strength that I never knew I had. It gives me the freedom to charge my worth and add tax. I am embracing my destined path of empowerment and self-encouragement. I once looked at myself for where I was but not for where God wanted me to be. I can now say I see me in my future, and I look even better than I do right now. I am excited about the greatness that I will continue to embark upon. I will leave you with this; remember to always first love you because you absolutely deserve it.

9.

Biography

Jasmine D. Milhouse is a Self-Love Transformational Coach, Motivational Speaker, Author, and Founder and CEO of LifeTipsbyJazz, LLC. Jasmine enjoys spending time with her husband and 3 children. She is a believer and knows her life would not be where it is without God. Her mission is to help women tackle their obstacles and oppositions to reconcile their self-love through personal coaching and daily strategies. Jasmine is also the author of How Did I Get Here: The Untold Journey of Finding Myself.

Before Jasmine started on her journey to help transform lives, the life she had to tackle first was her own. Being raised in a dysfunctional house can place anyone in a mentally turmoiled state. A lost traumatic little girl turned into a struggling, broken, hurt, and betrayed grown little girl. No longer wanting to be in her situation, she set out to transform her life with healing, forgiveness, mental uplift, and most of all self-love.

Hanging up the long hours of retail management for over 10 years, she discovered her true purpose for helping women. By building their self-confidence and self-esteem so they can go after the life of their dreams without ever having to seek anyone's approval with The Purpose to F.L.Y System™. Also, Jasmine hosts a weekly Facebook live show Life Tips by Jazz.

Purpose to F.L.Y. Clarity Session: lifetipsbyjazz.setmore.com

How Did I Get Here: The Untold Journey to Finding Myself

Facebook: Jasmine D Milhouse

Instagram: Life Tips by Jazz

Twitter: LifeTipsbyJazz

LinkedIn: Jasmine Milhouse

YouTube: Life Tips by Jazz

IV

Sparkle Taneka Robertson

10.

Dedication

I would like to dedicate my chapter to my grandmother Annie Evelyn Williams. My grandmother was born on January 23, 1937, three days before my birthday, January 26. She passed away on January 4, 2022. January has always been a prideful month for us; we would say that God had to start the year off right, that's why he created us!

My grandmother was a safe haven for me. She is where I ran to when I was afraid nervous, anxious, or just needed peace. Annie was a woman with very few words, but she always showed love through her actions. She never said "I love you" or "I'm proud of you," but I always knew she did through the grin on her face.

I dedicate this chapter to her because she taught me to push through life even when it seems like the world is against me. She taught me the importance of God, prayer, and church. It didn't matter how late I stayed out on Saturday night; I was going to church. She would knock on my bedroom door (our bedrooms were side by side) and say I know you just got in at 5 AM, but you're going to church. I would say I'm going to drive myself. Her reply, "No, you are not driving yourself. You better be ready at 10 AM because we will not be late." I would sleep the whole way to church. She was terrible at driving, just like me, because she taught me how to drive.

She instilled a determination in me that I can't put into words. Grandmama, I called her mama; I'm going to win this race called life for us!!! I love you, and I'm so proud to know that I have the best cheerleader in heaven, and her name is Annie Williams!!!! I see your beautiful grin, and I smell your beautiful aroma!

11.

My 1% Counts and Matters

When you think of one percent, most people might think that it is nothing. One penny, no thanks. One percent seems insignificant. In all actuality, the majority of my life, people looked at me and thought I was operating at 100 percent, while inside, I felt like one percent. I was miserable and depressed, down on myself and in life. I felt small. I didn't feel good enough. And most often, I felt unworthy. Even in moments of happiness, I felt moments of negativity magnified, dragging me down. I was miserable. Everything else was cover-ups. But once I started removing the covers, I felt myself becoming joyful, and it all started with a cheer.

One of the things I have done to overcome obstacles in life is to cheer myself on. You can even see it in my stance. When I take a picture, I put my arms out. I stand at attention. I fix my face. It's my way of saying, "You are victorious. You got this." Whenever I'm posing for pictures, I'm speaking life into myself, like I'm cheering on the team of me. That cheer came from a place of darkness.

My fairytale might not involve a glass slipper, but it does include overcoming to get to the other side of happiness. It involves real conversations with God and a long look at self. It's a concept many women might be able to relate to, maybe even the one reading this chapter. But before we get to the end, let's start at the beginning.

My mother gave birth to me when she was 15 years old. She was a good mother, but she had her own struggles, and while she did her best, children picked up on a lot of things. It started out as a seed, but eventually, from that experience, I gained a feeling of worthlessness that wouldn't let me go. Like a mean and unhappy friend, it followed me. I lived with a lot of family members during my life, and while many of them provided love and a roof over my head, a lot of them were trying to overcome. I found myself comparing my situation to more traditional families that compounded my feelings of worthlessness. My family showed me love, but because I had already made it up in my mind, I wasn't worthy; it didn't matter. I could have been a princess in a castle, but I still wouldn't have felt like royalty.

When I was in middle school, I went to live with my mother permanently. I didn't want to be there because there was so much going on in her house. It was busy. People often went in and out, and it was a hard place to be for a child needing attention. I never quite felt at home, so I would walk to my grandmother's house every day. It was my safe zone, and as the only child there, it was where I got my fix–attention. Attention to me meant love.

I also found love with other people. As a child, I would look most forward to the summers. That meant I could spend more time with my aunt, who treated me more like a daughter. To this day, I still call her my second mom. Her love showered me in our own little cocoon, and while it was a wonderful place for me, unfortunately, it still wasn't enough. The thing that kept sticking was my desire for attention. It became a deep want for me, a need. It would fuel my actions, my thoughts, and my interactions. I started to disappear in my need for attention, and that became my identity.

Because I didn't know who I was, I didn't trust anything that came out of my mouth. I had to copy other people. I loved how smart, pretty and cool my cousins were. Everyone liked them, but I took it a step further. I tried to repeat what they would say in the exact same way because I desperately wanted to be smart like them. As kids, my cousins and I, along with their friends, would walk to the store all the time. One of them would say something I felt was cool. A couple of minutes later, I'd try and say the exact same thing in the same way that they said it. I couldn't figure out who I was, and as a budding teenage girl, not having your identity can be very difficult.

I often would cry myself to sleep. I would look in the mirror and tell myself, "You're dumb. You're ugly. You're stupid." I would repeat the phrases like a mantra, and those words started manifesting. You know, the more you speak things into your life, the more weight they hold. I started believing them. While one normally might find attention in sexual relationships, my faith in God kept me reigned in. But my feelings of worthlessness did show up in other ways.

I wouldn't try out for teams because I had convinced myself that I wouldn't make it. I was the quiet girl at school. It wasn't because I didn't have anything to say, but because I felt like I wasn't cool enough to make friends. I would hang out with my grandmother all the time because I felt like I wasn't good enough to hang out with the kids at school. I put myself in this box.

Eventually, as I got older, it did get better. I tried to remove the box, but it was still there even throughout my relationships. Both in friendships and with people, I felt like the odd one out. Some situations magnified my feelings. I remember clearly my first love – my college sweetheart who gave me attention. He moved me out of my mom's house and into my own furnished apartment. He would take me out on dates and do things I had never received in other relationships. Sounds like a dream, right? I fell in love with his attention and him putting me first. It all felt like a fairytale until one day, it came crashing down. In the middle of one of our many conversations, he looked at me and told me he couldn't see me anymore. I was shocked. When I asked him why he went through a laundry list of things, all surrounding how his mother said I wasn't good enough for him. My love for bright clothes. How frequently I changed my hair. "She felt like you wouldn't be a submissive person," he told me when I heard that I wanted to commit suicide.

He went on and found someone else, a woman he had been with for years before me but apparently still wanted me to fight for his love. So much so that he gave me a call the night before his wedding. "Are you going to stop this?" he said. I don't know what he wanted me to do, but the damage was already done by that point. There it went again. I wasn't good enough, and I was tired of it.

I was tired of feeling small. I was tired of feeling like I didn't matter. I knew I had to get out of the city and go somewhere else. I couldn't just sit and watch him marry another woman, and I needed a fresh start. I wanted to get some kind of love. I wanted to be good enough for someone.

After that experience, I graduated from college and moved to Atlanta. I told myself, "I'm going to go somewhere where I only know two people because staying here will drive me crazy." At first, it was difficult living in a new city, but I eventually moved on and got my bearings. The career was going well, but I couldn't get to a full and happy place. I found love, gave birth to my daughter, and lived life. It was around this time I started changing.

Though I always knew who God was, It wasn't until I truly started developing a relationship with him that I really began to hear his voice. That took time, and it didn't happen overnight. In the meantime, I moved back home, found love, and got married. At that point, I felt like my life had reached an all-time high. Sometimes it felt like those old feelings of worthlessness had disappeared. But if you know one thing about life, it's that if you don't get to the root of a curse, it will continue to grow and manifest even if you can't see its flowers.

I was close to God, but I didn't know him in a sense. I attended church the same way I had the majority of my life, but in a way, I felt like I was faking. I didn't have an actual relationship with him. Fast forward, my husband and I started having problems. Our marriage ended in divorce, and those old feelings came back up once again. I fell back into this place where I was crying nonstop. This time, instead of thinking solely about being unworthy, I was also praising God in the middle of my tears. "I love you, Lord," I said, crying out to him. This time, he spoke back. He stopped me and said, "No, you don't." I was confused. "You don't even love yourself, and I made you," he said to me. "You can't be this much in love with me, and you don't even know the value of what I made." I was shocked and, at first, in denial. I battled back and forth with God. Could it be that in feeling unworthy, I truly didn't know who I was? I went to bed crying, upset, and hurt. The next day when I got up, I had reached an agreement with myself. I told God he was right. I didn't love myself, nor did I know who I was. I thought I was stupid. I thought I was dumb. I thought I was unworthy. I had so many negative thoughts about myself, but then I asked something that made all the difference in the world. I asked God the magic words. "Will you help me fall in love with me?" I asked for help.

Over the next few days, weeks, and months it was almost like God physically took my hand like a little baby. We took long walks every day, and he'd show me his beauty. "You see how I feed the birds. You see how I nourish the trees. In the same way, that's how I love you. Though the storm comes, the grass still grows. Even though all that you've been through, I still love you the exact same."

He started showing me his exact ways of love through nature on our long walks. One day he told me to look at the cracks of the sidewalk, where I found a bunch of ants. "Look down at them," he said. "You see how they're just enjoying life? They're crawling around, not knowing what comes, but they're enjoying life. They're doing their assignment. They're loving life. They're doing what they've been called to do. If I can love those little bitty ants, those specks of a being, just think how much I love you." I was completely floored.

It was like God was removing a veil from my eyes, and I could truly see. Even though I was literally going through hell, it was the first time in my life I had felt completely whole. I was going through a divorce. I didn't have a job. I was getting ready to get evicted from my house, but I was on a Cloud 9 with God.

It was around that time He started having me complete mirror exercises. He would tell me to look in the mirror and have me point to my body parts and tell me my self-worth. He would say, "Point to your eyes. Say, 'I love my eyes.'" I would repeat this from head to toe. I love my nose. I love my neck. I love my body. I love everything about me. I love Taneka Osborne Williams Robertson. He started telling me to say it out loud, and I would. In the mirror cheering myself on, I would say the words loudly."I LOVE ME! I LOVE WHO I AM! I LOVE HOW YOU MADE ME! I ACCEPT WHO I AM! I ACCEPT! I FORGIVE ME! I FORGIVE!"

It came out like a rainstorm. It was like a rebirth at the lowest point of my life. In the process of a divorce, with no money and a child to raise, I was speaking life like nobody's business. I was falling in love with myself. I was finding joy with myself, and suddenly my feelings of unworthiness were starting to fade. My tears were no longer tears, but they were like poms poms. Now, today I stand in a cheer mode all the time because, to me, I Got it. I'm running this race and winning. God is helping to see me through.

Even though I felt like one percent, I realized my thoughts and opinions mattered. My life mattered. One percent seems so small, but it's so big. You might have one tongue, but you can open your mouth and speak anything. You can have anything you want. It might not come right now. It might take time, but it will come. One thing about God is that he doesn't put you in a battle to lose. He gives you the capacity to carry what you need to carry. You are the apple of God's eye. He made you just how he made you. The trials and tribulations were a part of the process.

It took that low moment to truly realize all the ways in life where I had gone wrong and why nothing for me ever really succeeded. Because I didn't have the love and belief for myself, I couldn't trust myself to accomplish anything. I was covered and surrounded by love and people who wanted to support me, but I couldn't see it. The whole time my family loved me and tried to support me, but in my mind, I had already determined I wasn't good enough. I was failing and was so unhappy because the person I used to be wasn't who God intended for me to be. It was who I turned myself into. I wasn't succeeding because I wasn't truly being me.

To allow God to speak and work in your life, you have to be open. When you need help, you have to say you need help. You don't have to pretend you have everything together. The more you pretend, it delays your life's assignment. Now, I understand how you determine your destination. You have to go into life's battles like a prizefighter. When a boxer preps for a fight, they practice like they're winners before they even step into the ring. They speak life into themselves. You have to practice those techniques for your own life. If you're not speaking those same things to yourself when you go out to battle, you're going to lose. In order to go to God for anything, you have to trust yourself and trust that God will do what he said he would do. I carried this trust with me in my thoughts and spirit. I felt God transforming my mind. I found myself being truly honest. I was honest about how I loved myself, how I interacted with people, and even my hobbies. That failed attempt at joining the choir wasn't a reflection of my lack of effort. What I had to accept was that I'm not a singer. Everyone else could sing, so I tried, but that wasn't truly who I was.

Now, I do things I genuinely love and am truly good at, like creating my Sparkle4U Jewels Boutique. I know I will be great because I'm willing to put in the hours to make my business successful. Even if no one believes in it, I do. I call myself Sparkle Taneka Robertson because I worked hard for my Sparkle. Because I decided to be me and accept me, I was truly able to sparkle for myself. However, my sparkle isn't for me to try and copy anyone else like in my childhood. Neither is yours. My own sparkle matters. Your own sparkle matters. The world has to see you. You shine all by yourself.

Most jewelry pieces start with one little stone, but because you add pieces onto a necklace, it goes from one stone to a beautifully made design. That's similar to you. You are one little piece that came together to be this beautifully designed individual. To make things great, like a dish from scratch, you have to combine several elements. Each ingredient matters in a caramel cake. If you leave out the egg, it won't form right. If you leave out the yeast, it won't rise. If you leave out the butter, the cake won't taste as great. If you don't add a pinch of salt, then the flavors won't combine together. The same goes for a group of people. A team is made up of people, and each member on the team has an assignment. Each person has to play their role so they can defeat the opposition. No one can play soccer alone in every position. It's physically impossible. You have to come with your own uniqueness. You have to show up as a team, and each person has to play their role to make it work.

I used to wonder, "Why don't things ever work out for me?" Now I see it's because I went in thinking that they wouldn't. I convinced myself that my dreams weren't possible. I convinced myself I couldn't achieve, and you yourself might have fallen victim to the same actions. I felt like I spent so many years of my life trying to figure out how to lose until I decided to ask God for help. My 1% matters and counts because my opinion matters, my style matters, and my anointing matters. I count. I matter. You do too. You need others, but you matter. Without your 1%, you can't get to 100%, but you have to get to the one first and do the work. Everybody wants to be instantly great and have overnight success. We live in a microwave society, but that's not really realistic.

That's how it is in life. We all have to play our own part. That one part counts, and it matters to make everything work. We all can do great works because we all have unique gifts and anointing that God gave us. Your one idea can change the world. How do you get to be fearless and fabulous? You have to make up your mind to do so and become willing to make the adjustments. The number one might seem small, but 100 pennies make up one dollar. If you didn't count all those useless pennies, you would never reach one dollar.

If you could get anything from this chapter, from reading this book, I would say that I want you to believe in yourself. You matter. Your 1% counts. Life could not be possible without you. Go back and examine who you are, accept who you are, and forgive who you are. Put on your pom-poms and encourage yourself, and no matter how many times you've messed up or failed, you still cheer yourself on. Say the Cheer with me....My one percent counts and matters! Say it again...my one percent counts and matters. Now fill in the blank with your name. I,_____ count and matter! I can't hear you, say it a little bit louder. This is the one percent cheer.

If everyone came with their one percent, each one using their gifts and talents, their one percent would make an amazing team. You cannot get to one hundred until you decide to get to the one. If you think about the number one, you never see it limp or falling down. It always stands strong. So when thinking of yourself as one person, remember to stand tall. You. By yourself. Just the way you are, are important and matter. Carry that with you like a badge of honor, and never forget to share your sparkle with the world. Sparkle4U despite what life throws you! You deserve to Sparkle4U!

I always wanted life to be like a fairytale, and I didn't understand that you have to create your own. Every day I work to create my own happiness. I hope that you do the same.

12.

Biography

Sparkle Taneka Robertson is an entrepreneur, CEO, human resource professional, speaker, encourager, and motivator. She loves teaching people to sparkle despite what life throws them. Sparkle is a country girl with southern roots, love, and compassion for others. Sparkle Taneka Robertson is the daughter of Regina Williams and Timmy Osborne, Godparents Lisa, and Geno Demons. She is the mother of an amazing daughter named Alaysha Russell, a senior collegiate student at Alabama A&M University. Family is a factor in her life journey. Sparkle Taneka Robertson added Sparkle to her name after God taught her to sparkle despite what life throws her. She did not just develop this mindset for herself but stepped out in faith and started the Sparkle4U brand. Sparkle4U's mission is to build confidence, empower those they connect with by renewing their minds, hearts, and soul. Taneka "Sparkle" Robertson birthed this vision of adding the brilliant shine back into the lives of others while going through her transformation. She has a glowing personality of never missing a chance to smile. In her free time, she attends comedy shows, takes silent road trips, spends quality time with her daughter and friends. Her life passion is to leave sparkles wherever she goes.

V

Deborah Cooper

13.

Dedication

First and foremost, I would like to thank my Lord and Savior Jesus Christ for without him I am nothing. Forgiving me the ability and opportunity to bless others.

My Chapter in this Book is dedicated to the memory of my mentor, coach, and my friend

Kathy Elaine Jordon Pettus

"May she Rest in Peace"

Deborah Cooper

Fierce, Fabulous, and Free

14.

Being the Queen That I Am!

My name is Deborah Cooper; I am 58 years young. I am a woman who is all about inspiring and encouraging others. This has been in my DNA since birth. Growing up, I always had that take-charge spirit, but somewhere along the way, I lost it. I had no confidence in myself at all. Although my mindset had changed, I knew I was created to be a Queen, and it was time to take back my crown. I had to let some things and some people in my life GO! I no longer had time for the negativity. I realized my inner circle had to change. It was about me knowing my worth and walking in it, speaking affirmations daily, building my self-esteem back up, and taking better care of myself.

Being fierce is a process; it is getting a revelation and having the determination to grab your life and take action. To be fabulous, you must know your destination, the place where you would live out your greatness. Shifting your mindset is key. Know that you are equipped to do every dream that lives in your heart. Believe in yourself! It is time to step out and live the life you deserve. Don't just exist, live on purpose.

Even though I have a past and a history, I had to understand and trust that God has forgiven me and, most importantly, believe and forgive myself. I now use my story to help others because I refuse to be in bondage. God has equipped each one of us to succeed. We must reach down inside and trust the seed he has planted in us, water it, and grow. Now is the time to transcend your thoughts and beliefs about yourself and take the step to live the life you want. Work through your barriers and do what it takes to accomplish your goals. Sacrifice can be hard, but it's necessary.

Know your worth, Queen, then figure out how to act and proceed to walk in your Queendom. God wants us to be leaders and be creative in everything we do. We are powerful human beings. It takes lots of work and faith to walk in your mission and vision. It's actually a lifestyle, so, push yourself every day. It takes confidence and being fierce to be a Boss lady. I know my role as a wife, a mother, a grandmother, an entrepreneur, and a business specialist. I try to keep my focus on the prize. I am fabulous because I know how I feel about myself. I changed my mindset and my circle and now those changes are reflected in my lifestyle. I'm an influencer, and I have work to be done. Now, I am confident I can do all the things God has designed me to do.

I encourage you to be self-driven at a self-pace. Growth is good but care for yourself during the process. To truly operate in your freedom, you must set boundaries. I have been blessed to accomplish a lot through my skills by connecting myself and surrounding myself with positivity. I create my own atmosphere. I am a planner, and I get excited about what I am doing. My skills help me to pursue my purpose. I don't compete with anyone; I am free to be who I am. You should be excited about your journey too. We are all called to be great so learn to celebrate yourself. See, Queens are always genuine. You must let your yes be yes, and your no be no. You have the power to control your thoughts. Believe that you are an overcomer and a woman of integrity. Unapologetically go after your dreams and become unstoppable!

I challenge you today to think about these things. What does empowerment mean to you? What does Queendom mean to you as a woman? What is going on between your ears? What's happening in your heart? What's happening with your mindset – with the way you think? What are the words you are speaking out of your mouth? The bible says, "as the man thinketh in his or her heart, so he or she is." Sometimes your thinking has been broken by people, especially by men. Oftentimes it's people you trust. This is how I lost it before—through my desire to be accepted in life. My advice is to never beg anyone to accept you. When your mindset changes, the movement of your life changes. Romans 12:2 says, "Be not conformed to this world but be ye transformed by the renewing of your mind." Seek guidance from your heavenly father – your Creator. He makes all things new.

We must feed our self-esteem. There is a seed of Queendom in you, so start cultivating the mindset of being a true queen. We must interrupt the broken patterns and the noise in our life. Some of us need affirmations to build us up. Know what God says about you. The Beauty of having a relationship with God is that he shows us what to do and how to do it. The Holy Spirit shows us the value of the Crown. The value the creator has placed in us can never be broken. But we as queens must know our true worth. No matter what we have done in life, our value is still the same.

The mindset of a Queen is being secure in knowing who you are. When you are functioning in your right frame of mind, the mindset of dominion, you are not jealous of nor hating on anyone. Queens don't feel inferior to others. Once you adopt the true mindset of a Queen, it will be impossible for you to submit to anything less than what you believe or deserve. You can do whatever you choose. So, Queens, be Fierce, Fabulous, and Free, just like me. I make it my business to live my life to the fullest every day. I am living a Queendom life. Why? Because God says I can. He has equipped me to do so. You can do it too because God is no respecter of persons. Now stand up, get in your position, straighten your Crown, and get to work. Yesssss, I see you, Queen! Walk-in your Queendom.

15.

Biography

Deborah Cooper is a woman after God's own heart. A devout follower of Jesus Christ, wife, mother, mentor, motivational speaker, Spiritual Life Coach and Author. As a public speaker and life coach, Deborah passionately believes in the strength of the wife and shares her experiences of 39 years of marriage while caring for three wonderful children and four beautiful grandchildren. She has a passion to see women walk in their God-given assignment and purpose.

In Deborah's first published book: Prayer, The Power for Having a Successful Marriage she outlined how to work through the pressures of life as a woman and wife, with the goal of growing closer to God, which brings us closer to one another. Built to Last, Just the "3" of Us! is Deborah's second published book. Deborah has been collaborating with other phenomenal authors working on her 3rd Book called Rebirth of a Woman "Discover Unspoken Secrets" and her 4th book called I am a woman Empowered "A Book Anthology" Stories of Strength, Resiliency & Triumphs. Deborah attended The CAPP Institute "Coaching & Positive Psychology" where she received her Coach Training Intensive Certificate. Deborah also attended Kennesaw State University College of Continuing and Professional Education, where she received her Nonprofit Management & Administrative Certificates. She is presently in the process of receiving her Spiritual Life Coaching Certificate through the Holistic Learning Center.

Deborah is a Business Specialist under her business called H.A.T.S., LLC aka Having All To Stand. HATS is a consulting business. Her area of expertise is Virtual Assistant, Data Entry, and Bookkeeping.

Deborah is a Contributing Writer for the iShine Magazine. Her articles are focused on all marriages being Prosperous and Loving. The kind of marriage God intended for us to have.

Deborah has worked hard to make sure others are not stuck. She understands the importance of walking in your purpose and stepping out on faith. Praying and caring for people is her life. Her calling in the ministry is to be an intercessor for God.

Deborah is the founder/CEO of Let's Talk About It. Let's Talk About It is a Women and Marriage Enrichment Ministry, a vision that was given by God to reach and help save the lives of hurting women. Her business is set up to help and support married women of all faith, age, race, who are in search of a better and healthier marriage. She continues to create a safe and intimate atmosphere where women can share life experiences and seek the Word of God. A Place where women look toward Jesus Christ establishing a dependence on his Word knowing that God will bless their marriages.

Deborah focuses on issues that speak to your heart. To avoid becoming overwhelmed. To encourage women to be careful not to carry the weight of the world on their shoulders. To focus on what we can affect, and trust that other people will take care of the issues that matters to them—we are all in this together. She believes that Iron sharpens Iron. Deborah's Prayer is that all women- married or single be victorious in all aspects of their lives so we can help build God's kingdom together whole and complete.

Email: letstalkwithdeborah@gmail.com

coopdeborah@gmail.com

Facebook @letstalkwithdeborah

Instagram Deb_letstalkaboutit

iShine Magazine A&M Productions Contributing Writer

Ishinemagads.com

referral code   Ishine/Deborah

VI
Wanda Leonard

16.

Dedication

I would like to dedicate my first anthology to my Heavenly Father, God.

Lord, Thank You for being the head of my life, for being faithful, and for giving me my purpose, as well as showing me that I Am Worthy and Enough.

I would also like to dedicate this book to my loving husband (Anthony Leonard Sr.), my beautiful children (Anthony Jr., Andrew, and Ashari), my parents (Clyde and Linda Johnson, my siblings (Clyde Jr., Terri, and Aaron).

To my wonderful group of close girlfriends, you have saved me and poured into my life in more ways than you will ever know. I will love you forever. To my extended family and supporters, I see you, and I feel your love and prayers. I am forever grateful.

Thank you all for being in my life, believing in me, and helping me find my way through my most difficult challenges. Most importantly, thank you for teaching me how to love myself. I won't let you down, and I love you to the moon and back.

To those who suffer from some form of mental and physical illness, I pray my story helps you find your 'AH HA' moments and inspires you to turn your pain from a strain into a gain.

Remember to Be Brave, Be Bold, Be Mighty and continue to Be Blessed, my friend. We Got This!

17.

The Loud Silence

I consider myself to be extremely different from our perceived notion of normal. Because of that, many of my primary beliefs are quite simple, sound, and true….

hurt people will, most likely, hurt people,

everything in life is relevant,

everything happens for a reason,

every negative has a positive,

everyone deserves to be heard,

and everything that has happened to you has happened to someone else.

Most importantly, EVERYONE…absolutely everyone, experiences TRAUMA and PAIN!

The year 2009 will forever be etched in my mind. My life was complicated. I had just lost my job, we had moved to another state, and we were barely making it check-to-check as our family's needs steadily increased. I know, you are probably thinking, this sounds like a season out of anyone's life, right? Well, you are absolutely correct. Yet, for me, it was the beginning of something beyond my level of consciousness.

Oddly, I was extremely excited about the predicament we had found ourselves in. I wasn't overly concerned because we had been here a few times before. Only this time, I was not going to beat the pavement looking for the next opportunity to feel unappreciated by an employer and guilty as a wife and mom. I am a hustler by design. Along with my husband, the strategist, there was no way we would miss a beat. At least, that is what I kept telling myself as a daily affirmation.

Without a job, I was finally in a position to devote my time to becoming the "Real Housewife" I had desired to be. I could bake the cookies and have dinner ready when hubby arrives. I could help with homework and attend all of the school functions that I had missed so many times in the past. I was going to look the part too. I would wear cotton housecoats just like my Big Momma used to wear. You know the kind with the deep pockets and a zipper up the middle with strategically placed safety and bobby pins at your fingertips. Just thinking about how my Big Momma was somehow able to stuff her pockets with all of the essentials that anyone in the family could possibly need still amazes me to this very day.

At the time, we could have very well been homeless, and I would not have cared at all. I was tired of the rat race, traveling, and missing out as a parent. I was going to find a way to make things work out. After all, things had always worked themselves out one way or another—Every Single Time.

The significance of that year was that the word "HELP" came to me in a dream. It was so vivid and crisp that I could draw it, right today, in the same colors and intensity as it was in my dreams. As I awoke, all I remembered was just that word. No clarity! No insight! No direction! No reason! Just "HELP"! Not only was I very perplexed about the word, but I found myself becoming increasingly agitated at not knowing what it meant. I knew very well that God, "The Big Man" Himself, placed that word in my dreams. I just didn't know what He wanted me to do with it.

He and I had a very complicated relationship. Let's just say that's another story for another day.

This time was very, very different! He came to talk to me. I became so obsessed with the word "HELP" that I started to wonder if my dream was real. I had told the story to anyone and everyone who would listen. Each time I told the story, I became more and more agitated. I was secretly hoping the listener would give me the answer or, at the least, a hint. No one did. It was the weirdest thing. No one presented one hypothesis, hint, lead, suggestion, or advice. Absolutely Nothing!

I told that story for the next two years, thinking I was supposed to do something with it. Yet, I did not have a clue. So, I did what any person in my position would do; I became a super helper to any and everyone in need. I assumed that was what He wanted me to do.

My only request of God was to prevent me from exhibiting any signs of health issues around people outside of my immediate family. I put what I thought was His plan in motion. I began to HELP and invest in people as much as I possibly could. I also loved to spread joy and laughter to the people around me, always being the comedic relief to brighten someone's day. Saying 'No' was not an option......literally.

Being the eldest of four, the mother of three, and the aunt of many nieces and nephews, I availed myself to them and many others in the ways of being an ear, shoulder, comedienne, and voice of reason. I felt it was my calling to be available at a moment's notice. I came to the rescue most of the time without even being asked. I felt tremendous gratitude when helping others, despite being extremely uncomfortable when blessings were bestowed upon me in return.

Not only was I going to help others, but in the process, I was trying to become an even better person. Despite what I was personally going thru, life appeared to be good, and surely God was very pleased. I felt this way because I believed He kept the word "HELP" on my mind as a reminder of my purpose.

No one could have known that I was in a living hell. Physically and mentally, I was dying inside. My family witnessed my decline as I began to exhibit some serious health challenges that had become more and more difficult to manage as the years rolled by.

My overall health was deteriorating, and I was doing everything in my power to endure it without being exposed. All I needed was a correct diagnosis from the multitude of physicians and specialists that I consulted with for over 25 years. I wasn't going to complain to God about my health because I had already come to terms with my situation. I believed it to be my pre-destined burden to bare. After all, I believed it was up to the experiences and talents of my medical team to make me well again.

Imagine being in indescribable, full-body excruciating pain, fatigue and insomnia, severe anxiety, depression, brain fog, blurred vision, and fear each day. Now multiply that by a gazillion. This is the best way I can describe what it feels like. It is not a pretty sight.

As of 2009, I had been knowingly suffering physically for about 17 years and mentally for all of my life. I had become very skilled at being a master of disguise and a funny person. Even I didn't realize how many coping mechanisms I had put in place until they all began to crumble.

Exactly, how much trauma had I pushed out of my consciousness? At some point, I started to question whether some of my traumatic experiences had actually occurred. But I knew they had after the resurfacing of long-forgotten suppressed memories while in college.

I had become so skilled at being someone else that I completely forgot how to be myself. My mind and body were competing to determine which one would take me out first. It was apparent that they both were very strong contenders, and there would be no losers in this fight. I was losing my footing. Slowly but surely, my mindset began making the shift of self-hate, pity, shame, embarrassment, and regret.

What could I have done and, besides family, who could I have talked to and felt completely safe? Only my family and very close friends knew that I had to lie and hide what I was really going through. Even so, they were also in the dark and only later learned of just how bad it had gotten. I had no recollection of any childhood memories where we were being taught how to fight the demons that lived within.

I was raised during a time when self-care meant going to the hair salon, buying some new clothes, and getting your nails all prettied up. It was nothing like the world of today. There was no concept of learning to heal thyself through self-love. During my generation, we knew every form of trauma must be kept silent and never discussed. I eventually began to believe that strength was determined by the amount of trauma you could endure. Needless to say, most of the women from my childhood were some of the strongest women I had ever met.

I was raised to be a champion at everything I committed myself to. There was no room for tears and definitely no discussions about quitting. The rules were simple. Whatever happened in the past just happened. You are not to discuss it with anyone. Ironically, the households of many of my friends were no different than mine. In fact, many were more horrific. These experiences left me with a skewed view of the world.

The aftermath of my experiences didn't come to the surface until my college days. Thru experiences and observations of other females, I was conditioned to overlook anything traumatizing and move forward in life like it did not happen. Little did I realize, I wasn't as so-called strong as I once thought. It would all come to a boiling point, and my life began to spiral rapidly, out of control.

From 2009 to 2012, I was doing everything in my power to stay alive. Unbeknownst to anyone else, enduring the pain and other health issues while trying my hardest to maintain my sanity was becoming completely impossible. I became sicker and sicker with each passing year. Also, with each passing year, the word "HELP" resonated just as vibrant as it had when it first appeared.

More insight regarding the word "HELP" came to light in 2012. By that year, I had another vision. This one informed me that I had about five more years before something major would happen. I knew the feeling all too well. It was the same nauseating feeling that would make me rise straight up in the bed and proceed to experience what one would call debilitating panic attacks. Almost always, my vision was correct. I had absolutely no reason to doubt my 5-year contract would indeed expire.

It came to me so crisp and clear that I found myself, once again, telling the story to anyone who would listen. This time, I began to question whether I was doing what God was clearly instructing me to do. Maybe, I'm supposed to do something else with the word "HELP?" Just Maybe! This game of charades was definitely nerve-wracking at best.

Right about the time I received this vision, I had just landed another great job. It was a dream job that basically fell in my lap. In terms of work, I had my career path all worked out. It was going to be difficult, but my mind, body, and spirit had to take a backseat to my passions and purposes while I chased that all-mighty dollar. I was extremely happy that my new job would help move my family from state to state. We were going to be starting all over again. By this point, we had become gypsies anyway. So like always, I was excited about the upcoming chance to reset.

Yet, this time, I had a little hesitation because this move felt different…. significantly different. I often ponder whether I should have left the money on the table and remained where I was? In hindsight, that move and the many years to follow were absolute hell.

I had gotten to the point where I could not do much physically, so I had to rely on my extended family for assistance. I would have rather been shot in the ass than to have to ask for help. My kryptonite had been discovered. Oh, No, God! Please tell me "HELP" does not mean I have to be on the receiving end of assistance. At this point, I realized how much effort I had been putting into controlling my environment and suppressing my emotions. I knew this move was the beginning of the storm.

My ability to hide my pain was breaking down. My smile was not as bright, my emotions were raw, my ability to bounce back was not as quick, my senses were deteriorating, and my mental health was nose-diving. I began to wonder whether God was actually the one becoming agitated with me. Although I wasn't entirely clear about what He was instructing me to do, I do know that there were times when He gave me very clear visions that eventually came to fruition. Why would I doubt what He was asking me to do this time?

I felt lonely, angry, misunderstood, and completely empty. I was certain of two things. I was not carrying out His vision for me, and I only had five more years to get it together. Being faithful to my instructions, I proceeded to tell my husband to prepare to be the sole provider for the family because God had informed me that I only had a limited amount of time before something major would happen. I did not know what would occur, but I knew it would probably be the ultimate test of my existence. I had no more fight left in me. Within those five years, I endured 11 surgical procedures, fought breast cancer, lost my father, endured countless injections and nerve ablations, attended therapy sessions, and took more medicines than I can ever share. Let's just say one entire drawer in the nightstand was just for my meds, and it stayed packed.

As morbidly as it sounds, I was convinced that one way or another, I had about five more years before it would all be over…..like Over! Over! Sadly, the mere idea was somewhat gratifying. At least, I wouldn't be damned for taking myself out; somehow, it would be conducted for me. Surely, God would not allow me to hurt forever. Would He?

By the end of 2012, my doctors were convinced that my plethora of health problems would be things of the past if I would just elect to have bariatric surgery. I had reached a weight of 336 lbs. and the surgery was beginning to sound like a brilliant plan.

On the day of the surgery, I sat in the waiting room, wanting to run out of the door. I clearly remembered a friend telling me that I didn't have to proceed with the surgery. Initially, I thought she was not convinced it would help me. Neither did I, but eerily, it was something about the way she said it. I had this strange feeling that she was channeling a message that was not of her own thinking.

It had become too much to always see my loved ones concerned and worried about me. They couldn't help me, and they felt useless. Being as I felt like a huge burden to the family and a failure, I owed it to my family to try something...anything. The looks of hope I saw in their faces were too much to handle. So I proceeded with the surgery. As luck would have it, I lost 133 lbs. within a year. I should have been happy and relieved of my many ailments. Unfortunately, I was not.

At my much smaller size, my pain had gotten worse. I found myself dealing with additional health challenges due to only being able to eat a few bites of food and a few sips of water before I was curled over in excruciating pain. Once again, my family felt helpless. Besides going to work, I rarely left my bed and developed daily bouts of severe anxiety attacks and major manic depression.

My family couldn't HELP me.

Many of my friends started to alienate me and seemed to have become distant. They couldn't HELP me.

My employer reprimanded me for my excessive sick days and for not being the over-working, self-hater that 1 had become known for. They couldn't HELP me.

I became very resentful, angry, and sick…very sick. I couldn't HELP MYSELF!

Thus, the spiraling continued.

By 2017, I had endured the majority of my medical procedures. I had so many medical professionals that I was certain they would eventually name a wing of the hospital after me. I began to disengage with many of my friends and members of my family and became more introverted. For the most part, I was experiencing difficulty in my memory, sight, and hearing and was experiencing embarrassing uncontrollable hand trembling. The gig was up! I was no longer physically and mentally able to engage in social activities and do the job that I educated myself to do.

Imagine living in a world where you were in a constant battle with yourself. Your mind and body are both in a state of torture, and every single day you endure warfare of horrific proportions. Living with chronic pain often means managing a huge weight of emotions and constantly trying to explain the unexplainable.

By 2018, I was couch-bound. I couldn't even sleep in my customized orthopedic bed due to the indescribable pain that covered every nerve, muscle, and bone in my body. I had to be assisted with basically everything. As I wallowed in my pitiful state of being, I began rationalizing my existence and purpose in life. At times, I had become debilitated and paralyzed from the overwhelming and increasing complete loss of control. How in the world was I going to fake it until I made it when my well had run dry?

The truth of the matter is I was DONE! I spent the majority of my days planning…Always Planning! Death just made sense! It was a natural thought. One that I knew intimately well.

No more pain! No more burden! No more crying! No more worrying! No more apologizing! No more explaining! No more Self-Destruction! NO MORE ME! For the first time that I can recall, I took off my gloves, let down my walls, and succumbed to defeat! Never, ever have I been backed in a corner without being able to come out swinging. I began to be happy that my father was not able to witness my decline. That would have killed me for sure. Yet, I felt his presence around me all of the time and was convinced he already knew.

All I could think of was the rationale and the necessity of what I was about to do. I WAS DONE! DONE! DONE!

I have nothing more to prove! I will no longer be a burden, and I will be in no more pain. I convinced myself that I was making the best decision because surely no one was expecting me to endure this forever. I could not muster up the thoughts of living with it even one more year.

Then, once again, I heard God!

This time, God said, "STOP! WHAT ABOUT ME???" As loud as I could, I shouted over and over, "What about you?" Each time laughing and crying louder and louder.

All I kept hearing was the word "HELP" in repeat mode.

I stood there looking at myself, crying. It dawned on me that I had not looked at myself like that before. After staring clear thru to my soul, I became overwhelmed with joy, shame, and embarrassment all at the same time. As if nothing had ever happened, I put the pills back in the bottle, stumbled to my place on the couch, and held my precious dog. All the while, praying feverishly that God would send me the answers as to how I was going to know more about Him and love myself enough to take my life back. Basically, how was I going to heal?

The only response I received was "HELP"!

I have pondered and struggled for years trying to define my 2018 journey in a succinct way that minimally clarifies it in its entirety. I have finally resolved to simply state it was beautiful, it was scary, it was lonely, and it was life-changing.

As time went on, I no longer had suicidal thoughts, and I learned more about my conditions. Although my rap sheet of conditions was embarrassingly lengthy, it was Fibromyalgia (myalgic encephalomyelitis/chronic fatigue syndrome (ME/CFS)), which took me out. I became relieved to know that all of my symptoms were valid and my health problems all had names. After having poor health for so long, I was conditioned to believe I only imagined the severity of the pain. I also learned the host of medications I was taking were only masking the pain and damaging several other areas of my body.

By 2019, I learned how a person's mental state is directly connected to their physical state. I never even considered the correlation between my mind and body. I understood why my body possessed these irreversible health issues. They were due to years of unresolved and unacknowledged trauma, high stress, and self-destructive habits. Another thing I realized was, in a way, I was keeping myself in a debilitated state because I constantly tried to prove that something serious was wrong. Yes, this was my year of discovery. I was losing weight and determined to change the trajectory of my life.

If I were going to co-exist with these symptoms for the rest of my life, at least I would educate myself enough to fight back. I had done everything I thought I was supposed to be doing, but I was still haunted with feelings of not fulfilling God's ultimate plan for me.

God instructed me to STOP and put the primary focus on myself. I felt selfish and had a little bit of regret, but I knew I had to do what I was instructed to do. I stopped, but only under one condition. I needed to know why? Was I chosen, or was I cursed? I built up the courage to ask Him the question I had feared to ask him all of my life.

"Why Me Lord?"

Then, just as clear as I write these words, He exposed Himself and feverishly played back the story of my life. I watched a movie that spawned from as early as two years old.

I was shown how everything I had ever experienced was for a purpose. Absolutely everything prepared me for my huge tasks ahead. God and I talked for hours on end. I realized during the course of my life that He had always been there. ALWAYS!

I even began to vividly recall moments when I had experienced extreme trauma, and He would not allow me to buckle and fold. There were times when I thought I had developed coping mechanisms to forget traumatic events, but He was able to show me that He was there talking to me and protecting me all of the time. I didn't have coping mechanisms. I was just me being the way He had designed me to be. He poured into me a purpose that I don't believe I have enough life to fulfill. Yet, I still have to accomplish as much as I can.

All of my questions were answered. He laid out a plan for me, unlike any map a person can even begin to conceive. He went so far as to show me what the rest of my life could look like with Him leading the way. I began to see everything for what it was and what it could be.

Even with the catastrophic events and loneliness of 2020, I was still able to understand why I was stagnant and not flourishing in life. He pulled me out of a state of calamity and literally moved all distractions and barriers out of my way. I no longer had excuses and escape routes. I just had to start somewhere. He allowed me to fail and restart time and time again. Each time, I learned why I failed and to distinguish when I was not allowing myself to be led.

This was when I allowed myself to pull back, stop moving, and seek silence. It was in the silence when the answers became loud and clear. Everything I thought I was doing right was wrong. I was supposed to do the work needed on myself and carve out time for Him. Yet, I had long since stopped talking to Him and was trying to do everything but focus on myself. The battle was not mine to fight. I was supposed to take it to Jesus and leave it, but not one time in the past did I give my troubles to Him and walk away.

I never even considered silence as being something I would eventually cherish and crave. There was a time when I hated the silence. It was in the silence when my senses had to be very keen. It was in the silence that my resilience and determination could not waiver. It was in the silence when I felt most unloved. It was in the silence that I first experienced intense pain. I never knew so much could be heard when things were quiet. Without a forced quarantine in the year 2020, I don't believe I would have ever prioritized my life in a way to carve out time for myself to be spiritually and mentally nourished.

The hopes for my future were clearly bright. God helped me realize He was always in control. He had been sending his angels my way for all of my life. In 2020 alone, I began to mysteriously receive calls, texts, private messages, and cards from people I barely knew. They were all encouraging me to stay the course because I had a job to do. Many times the message was simply, "I see you and your heart. Trust in the Lord to carry you through." It was freaking me out because my answers were all around me. My purpose for the word "HELP" was finally fully defined.

God had forced me to come to Him. He showed me that He was the only way. I learned the skills and practices of spending time with Him thru prayer and meditation. I realized that most of my health problems were caused by traumatic events and acts of self-destruction and self-neglect. He literally put me to the test in more ways than I can share in this instance. Just know there is always a lesson to be learned in everything. The key is to process it with God in silence. Eventually, the answer will present itself loud and clear.

I was once told, "People will treat you how you treat yourself." and "People will treat you how you allow yourself to be treated." As simple as these two statements seem, I found them to be very profound and accurate. I quickly understood they summed up my life perfectly.

It was no one else's fault nor responsibility to fix me, but ME!

People are people, and everyone has their own road to travel. I could no longer harbor any hurt from the past. When I came to the conclusion that there are things that I just cannot control, I stopped placing many additional obstacles in my way—particularly the ones that hadn't even occurred. I am learning to stop claiming all of the negative things that could go wrong and celebrate all of the things that will be right.

Now, I view my health issues as superpowers. I learn something from every single nerve in my body. Can you even imagine knowing how much POWER I must possess? To think, I am only just getting started. Who knows, I may save the world!

My point here is to say, as with any power, you have to learn to use it for good. So, instead of detaching from the world so that I would not be remembered, I am now driven by my purpose and self-preservation needs so that my imprint on this world would not be forgotten.

Most importantly, I learned that I mattered, I'm blessed, I'm enough, and I'm highly favored. It is very freeing to allow God in your life. It has not been easy, by no means. Life can be very difficult and hard to navigate, yet it can also be as enjoyable, fruitful, and rewarding as you will allow it to be. I now appreciate every second of my experiences and existence because it makes me the woman that I am today.

So, remember when I mentioned that I was not normal? I often wonder what it feels like to be normal. Does it have a taste, a smell, a sound? Oh, I get it; it's a look. Certain kind of look, right? Hmm, that can't be because we are all unique, distinct, and rare. Not to even mention, we are all individually designed. Yeah, I am definitely not normal, nor do I ever wish to be.

I was once told I had to be healed to heal others. I do not believe that because healing is a never-ending process. As long as I am in pursuit of healing, I am becoming more prepared and experienced to be that person to meet people where they are and understand where they have been. You have to believe in the possibilities and know that you are the most precious jewel on the earth. It is up to you to keep yourself polished and sparkling. Afterwards, you have to go for it without any reservations.

I have learned to be brave, bold, and mighty through my journey.

I must be brave to be fierce.

I must be bold to make myself feel fabulous even when I don't think I can.

I must be mighty to break every chain that tries to prevent me from being free.

Now, I absolutely love the newly improved Fierce, Fabulous, and

Free Me. I have learned my purpose in this life is to "HELP" in every way possible, starting with myself.

18.

Biography

Wanda Leonard is an emerging motivational influencer, speaker, author, and entrepreneur. She advocates for better prevention and awareness programs for people who suffer from chronic pain and mental health illnesses. After spending a lifetime suppressing traumatic experiences and disguising her severe health decline, everything came to a complete halt in December of 2017. She found herself surrendering to a complete mental and physical breakdown. After consideration of suicide in 2018, Wanda made the vital decision to thoroughly understand the root causes of her plethora of illnesses and identify ways to manage them more effectively.

Through her discoveries, Wanda worked with a dedicated and compassionate team of medical professionals who were just as driven to the solutions as she was. Wanda was introduced to the need for routine mental therapy, implementation of self-care solutions, and practices of spiritual and mindful techniques. Wanda has committed herself to teaching others how to identify stress and pain triggers; as well as, behaviors that may be contributing to their mental and physical day-to-day struggles. These days, if you don't see Wanda educating and advocating for causes such as post-breast cancer support, mental health/chronic pain awareness, and medicinal marijuana reform, she will be somewhere with her support system and inspiring others to reclaim their lives. She is dedicated to helping save lives from suicide and self-sabotaging behaviors by promoting more patient involvement, better illness identification, proper education, and reform for more natural medicinal solutions for chronic pain and mental illness.

VII

Charlotte Gillespie

19.

Dedication

I am dedicating this chapter to my grandmother and grandfather: A woman and man that Inspired me, pushed me, encouraged me, and loved me throughout all of my life.

To my grandfather, who is deceased, I'm here making you proud.

My grandmother is still here to witness my story. Without God and my grandparents, I would not have made it this far to tell my story.

20.

Healing a Broken Heart

There are so many moments in life where you just want to give up and throw in the towel. It feels as if you don't know your worth, and you don't know if it's even worth fighting for, if it's even worth the push. Fourteen years ago, I lost the most special person in my life next to my mother, the woman that pushed me, supported me, loved me, cared for me, and most of all, raised me. After her death, I practically gave up on everything. I was still in middle school, and everything started falling apart from there. I was no longer interested in classes or anything pertaining to school. I knew that I had a future, but it was hard not to allow myself to give up.

I was always a church girl, but the church became just church to me after her death. I stopped wanting to be an active member. It felt like I was going just because I had to. At that point, I knew it was not me. So, I began to fast and try to strengthen my relationship with God. I prayed for strength and courage to carry this weight on my shoulder. As years passed after her death, I realized I was not applying and pushing myself as I should. I felt that no one was giving me the push that I needed to move forward.

In 2011, I graduated from High School, and it was time for college life. I could not and did not want to face what was next in my future. I knew that my family wanted what was best for me and wanted me to move forward and be the young lady God called me to be. I did not wish to proceed further in the state of mind I was in. I was not interested in college at the time, but I did it anyway. I attended Northwest Community College, staying on campus, thinking it would be a relief not to be around the same people every day.

Those thoughts didn't last long. Eventually, I stopped attending any of my classes. I slept a lot, and nothing or no one interested me. Initially, I roomed with an unusual young lady; however, I moved because I believed she was mistreating me. I really just wanted to be alone, in my own space, and in my own world being me. After moving out of the dorm, I realized it was not her. It was the mental state that I was in. All I wanted was music, sleep, food, and my phone. I was literally at the point of doing whatever I had to do to be in peace, to rest, and to be happy. Happiness was rarely a state I was ever in. I could not be happy to save my life.

I was dealing with all types of emotions, especially anger. All I wanted was to be alone. I really did not want to tell anyone what was occurring because, in my mind, no one cared. I wanted to give up on everything and everybody, but I kept going with a smile. I hid all of the hurt, pain, discomfort, anger, dissatisfied thoughts, and feelings that I felt. Feelings of not being worth it.

Since I was not in the mood for college, I applied for a job at a daycare. I realized after the first semester that it was time for me to come home. I was not feeding my brain the knowledge it needed because it did not interest me. I explained to my family how I needed to come home because college was not for me at the time. After leaving college life, I started working at my church's daycare. Working at a daycare or in a school with children was my passion. I loved and still love children. I thought working full-time hours would help, but during nap time, when there wasn't any action, my mind started thinking about the fact that this was my career choice as a child. After working seven years in a daycare, I pursued my career and received my childcare director/owner license.

I was proud that even in a difficult state of mind, I was still able to pursue my career and do what I needed as far as my education. I knew I was starting a career that I loved.

I'm a young lady who loves children, and through it all, that job suited me well and eased my mind. The career motivated me to go to school and take classes in childcare development. Eventually, that shut down for me. I was upset and humiliated because that was what I loved doing. It was the one thing I knew I had, and that was the degree that it took to keep going and go higher.

I stayed home for a while and took care of my grandmother. It was a task being depressed, angry, antisocial, and more. I made it through with God leading and guiding me. It was not easy for either of us. My prayer life and relationship with God became closer than ever. Even with the prayer and connection, I still felt that I was not the woman I needed to be. I started feeling that I was worthless and that feeling lasted a couple of years afterward. Three years passed before I started feeling like the woman I needed to be; God finally answered my prayers.

I believed that God had turned that test into a testimony.

I felt relieved.

I felt that I had accomplished a goal.

I felt that I had done great work.

I felt proud and accomplished.

I felt that I am somebody; I am worth it.

I felt fabulous.

Years after coming to myself and being the woman I was called to be, death struck again. I wanted to go back into the same state of mind and give up on everything. I tried to isolate myself from everyone and tune everything out. I knew I could not allow myself to relapse into that state of mind. It was the passing of my grandfather that took me back to that place. He was my biggest supporter, motivator, and leader. I worked for my grandfather for years as his secretary from the age of 8 up to the age of 13.

Death wasn't something I wanted to experience again. It came too soon – this time, I had to continue working and gain more hobbies to ease my mind and accept the death. I knew it had to end because I realized death had an effect on me; it bothered me a lot and in so many ways. I prayed two to three times daily that God would ease my mind and not let me go into depression. I knew I was headed to that point even though I worked hard to occupy my mind to be able to accept the deaths that were occurring.

I started small businesses to let me know that I was worth it, that I'm fabulous, that I'm able to move on and move forward. After starting the small business, I began to know where I stood, what my occupation was, and what I was put here to do. I didn't realize I had the knowledge and skill to do as much as I could since I allowed stress, depression, and anger to overtake me. I understood the assignment.

In 2021, a year after the pandemic hit, I decided to tell my story, my testimony, thinking it would ease my mind. I realized I had to go from the beginning and carry my story (my testimony) step by step. Even through the deaths, disappointments, hurt, discouragement, pain, and discomfort, I knew that I had a story to tell. The world needed encouragement. I knew so many people were going through the same illness, same situations, and battling the same mental state. They needed someone to encourage them with a similar or same story. My story not only encouraged others, but it also encouraged me as well.

It brought about another journey to let me know I am fabulous and

I have something worth living for. Now I had a way to help myself and others. There were so many times during those years I wanted to just leave this world because I thought I would be at peace. God said, "No, it's not your time. I have more in store for you." As I wrote my story, it made me realize everything I had gone through, everything that had my state of mind where it was. It brought times of my own illness as a baby with a grave illness. I looked myself in the mirror after remembering all of that and said to myself, "I AM BLESSED." After all, I've been through, after all of my thoughts and feelings at the time, God allowed me another chance; I am Blessed.

As I continued to encourage the world through writing, I encouraged myself as well. I didn't go through a grave illness, see and suffer the deaths of my loved ones, and so much more if I was not worth it, if I was not fabulous, and if I was not fierce. I knew my entire family was aware of my story. They knew about the pain, the illness I went through, and they were there for me, but it no longer felt that way after those two deaths. My aunt and grandfather knew how I stayed in Critical Care for 30 days, how the doctors gave me up to leave this world as an infant, how I survived being an ECMO baby …an ECMO Baby is where your stool backs into your lungs and poisons your whole system. The doctors say the baby won't live long with this disease. I'm 28 years old, and I'm still here. I carried myself through it all with the help of the Lord.

I continued those thoughts, revisiting that journey when my job closed down. It was a job that I loved; my passion was to work with children. I felt that working with children daily eased my mind. I stayed busy working with children, whether it was teaching or being the director. Their smiles, the learning time, and the social time allowed me to not think about my situation. I was at peace. I worked in childcare seven of those years that I was troubled. After the closing, I felt myself going back. Those were the moments I took on other businesses, hobbies, and other goals. I became Charlotte Gillespie again. I stayed that woman of courage even through the pandemic. I realized how fierce and fabulous I was and that I was worth it.

Once again, I learned of another death. I did not let this one bother me as before, but it gutted me because he was my father. Sadly, I never met him in all of those years; I never knew him. I did have the opportunity to talk to him once. Six years after speaking to him, I wanted to know more about him only to get the news that he was deceased. I learned more than I expected; I found out how many brothers I had, my father's sisters, and so much more. I had to also learn that he died of cancer. I never knew while he was alive that he was sick.

It hurt me badly that I did not know who he was. It bothered me to know that I grew up without him being a father to me. He never told any of his family about him having another daughter until after he found out he had cancer, and it wouldn't be long before he left this world.

Through the process of the two deaths, my illness, and everything else that I struggled with, I did not have him there to be the father that I needed in life. The one time I talked to him before his death, he told me to call him by his name; I wanted to call my father "daddy," honestly, but he did not allow me the opportunity. I had to pray the prayer of forgiveness many times.

It was hard knowing that I didn't have that father figure in my life. It was hard knowing that through trials and tribulations, pain, heartaches, and tears that he was not there to encourage, comfort, and pray for me. I knew I had my mother, but to have both would have been a lifesaver. Not only did I suffer through the deaths, not only did I suffer an illness, not only did I get to suffer an unhealthy state of mind, depression, anxiety, but I also suffered the lack of parental love. During the moments I had my grandfather, I didn't know and realize how much I needed a father figure because he was always there. He gave me what I needed and wanted. After his death was the moment I realized I needed my father. Those times of looking for him, I was eager, but after knowing of his death, I was depressed. My state of mind went back to being in depression mode.

I wanted to once again give it all up, but I knew the love that God gave me and the love that surrounded me. I had to strive to keep going; If it was not for God being by my side and somebody praying for me, all of this could have gone another way. Even after the trials and the illness, I wanted to take peace further but in the wrong way. I had to continue my small business and hobbies. My mind had to stay occupied and controlled. Every time I thought it was all going well, something else would slap me in the face; I would always fall back into the same cycle. All of the times I would get back to the woman that I needed to be, something would knock me down.

Each of these moments made me feel that I was not worth it. Instead of feeling fabulous, I felt all fear. Fear, depression, anxiety, and a troubled mind hit. I could not win for losing in my eyes. Others thought differently of me, but I could not see it or feel it. I was just at a loss…

I experienced a close to death situation, two traumatic deaths, being without a father, learning of his death, and more. It was challenging to find the courage to move forward. I didn't finish college; I worked to get into the career path I wanted and desired; I needed that college degree; I needed that career choice; I needed that courage, prayer, and love; most importantly, I needed the prayers.

In the mental state I was in, I needed the prayers. At the end of the years of riding the roller coaster, prayer is how I made it. There is power in prayer. Through the difficult moments,

I never stopped praying; however, my faith is what I did not apply. Faith is the substance of things hoped for and the evidence of things not seen. I was not seeing anything happening for me that was right. Praying without believing did not work. I had to believe after praying in order for God to work on my behalf. I not only had to pray and believe, but I also had to help myself. I had to want to do what was needed to get out of that mental stage; I had to want to live and become a better person.

Becoming a fierce, fabulous person of worth was not easy... it took work. I made it!! I thank God for helping me make it. I thank him for a kept mind, a praying family, praying leadership, and a few praying friends. I had a tribe that I turned away from because of my thoughts and feelings. I had to know my worth in life to believe everything else. I finally had the chance to know my worth, to know who I really am. and to know that I can conquer anything in life. All of it taught me that if I passed these tests, I could pass whatever is brought before me in life.

I encourage all ladies to know your worth, even in the seasons where you are troubled, down, ill, unloved, or alone. You are worth it; you are fierce, fabulous, and free. You are the woman that God called you to be. You are the woman that's able to say that "I'm still standing and ready to encourage the world!" It's the troubles and trials that provide a lesson, not always the good things in life, that show how strong of a woman you are. It's not always the good that tells your testimony or allows you to help others. At my lowest moments where I could not help myself, I was able to help others. I was able to encourage others because I had a story to tell. I had words, knowledge, and proof to tell them how and what to do. There are moments when you're feeling down and out, or when you're feeling discouraged and disappointed that you're not the woman you intend to be. In those moments, remember to know your worth and that you are fierce, fabulous, and free!

21.

Biography

My name is Charlotte Gillespie, I am 28 years of age. I was born and raised in Olive Branch, Ms… I am the sister of 5 brothers; 1 by my mother and 4 by my father. I graduated from Olive Branch High School… attended college at North West Community College. As I attended school I worked for my grandfather as he owned Gillespie Trucking… I was his secretary for 8 years. I received my education in childcare development. I became a certified childcare director… as well as worked in a Childcare Center for 7 years. After working in childcare I began writing. In May of 2021, I released my first book entitled "I Survived", a personal story/ testimony about myself. Now I am into the business of credit repair… Gillespie Financial, LLC is launching. The book tells the story of why I am the young lady that I am today. I am currently working on marketing, starting my own daycare as well, and being a better me.

VIII

Jamaica Townsend

22.

Dedication

I would like to dedicate my chapter to my husband and children. Thank you for always believing in me and supporting me in all that I do. I pray that I have been a good example to demonstrate that through Christ you can do all things. You can do anything that you put your mind to. I encourage everyone to always keep God first, follow your dreams and be at peace.

23.

I am who you say I am: My Journey to finding my identity

"I am who YOU say I am.... My journey through finding my identity in Christ led me to be empowered, fierce, fabulous, and free."

Who are you? Growing up, we think we know who we are, and we do have a better understanding of who we are at those tender young ages. Early in life, most of us have pure and innocent thoughts of who we are because we have not been tainted by the world's opinions of who we are. As we grow older, we tend to accept and receive negative perceptions of ourselves based on other people's opinions. This leads us to consciously or unconsciously take on an identity that does not belong to us. At this point, we continue to go through life trying to "find ourselves." Man, what a journey that can be! We find ourselves having difficulty answering the questions: Who are you? What defines you? What is your identity? Too often, we hide behind titles and use them to identify ourselves when those titles are not who we are at all. Those titles are merely what you do, not who you are. God wants us to find our identity in Christ. We waste time trying to find our identity in things and in relationships rather than looking to Christ alone.

If you happen to have been blessed with a good family, you were encouraged and inspired to be the best version of yourself that you can be. Growing up, I was always told that I was beautiful, intelligent, had great potential, and had a bright future. I constantly had good words spoken over me as a child and even into adulthood. At some point along the way, I stopped believing those words that were spoken about me. You see, the enemy comes in to steal, kill and destroy (John 10:10). He comes to plant lies in your head about your identity. One of the first seeds he purposefully planted into my life was the negative spirit of fear. Fear is false evidence appearing real. The enemy is a liar! It is one of the enemy's favorite tools to keep us from moving forward. Fear will paralyze and stagnate your life.

"The heart thinks! Therefore, if the enemy can bombard you with thoughts that produce fear and anxiety, he can then remove your ability to manifest the will of God in your life." Chuck Pierce

I have to remind myself that God did not give me the spirit of fear, but power, love, and a sound mind (2 Timothy 1:7). He made me think that I was inadequate and not qualified or brave enough to do specific things publicly. He tried to make me believe that I could not make an impact in the world. He tried to make me believe that I was unloved. He tried to make me believe that I would not be successful in life. He tried to make me believe that I was weak and would never measure up. He tried to make me wear a mask and cover up who I really am. He tried to make me believe that rejection was my portion.

Once my eyes were opened to see the schemes of the enemy, my mindset had to change. I had to renew and transform my mind and seek who God says I am. I had to stop believing the lies of the enemy and become an advocate for my own life. I no longer allow myself to self-sabotage and self-destruct by agreeing to the lies. I had to get rid of the limiting beliefs. I had to saturate my mind with God's word, which is the truth, and come to the realization that his love for me is unconditional. The journey to finding a healthy identity has not been easy, but I am so grateful for every failure and every struggle. This journey has caused me to do a deep soul search to find my identity in Christ and understand what being empowered, fierce, fabulous and free really looks like.

I am now empowered because my God-given purpose in life is to empower, encourage and inspire others who may be struggling to find their identity by being transparent about my own life experiences. We must realize that our pains, struggles, rejections are not for us; they are our testimony for others. Even if I just touch one life, I have fulfilled my purpose in the earth for God's glory. I thank God for using me as his vessel to empower, encourage and inspire others to walk in their God-given purpose. In 2016, God gave me a vision to start a women's group. For such a long time, I did not call it a ministry (knowing that is what it was) because I did not feel qualified (another trick of the enemy), but I knew I had to be obedient because I had given God my "Yes" to serve him. I had to stand on his word because God did not give me the spirit of fear, but power, love, and a sound mind (2Timothy 1:7) and "Fear of man will prove to be a snare, but whoever trusts in the Lord is kept safe." (Proverbs 29:25, NIV).

When he gave me the vision, he did not provide all the details, as that is how he operates. Because I didn't have all the details, the enemy planted more seeds of deception, fear, procrastination, and double-mindedness. He caused me to second guess whether God had even told me to do this. He put negative doubting thoughts in my mind like, "What if I fail? What will others think? Can I even do this?" In spite of those doubts, I had to put my trust in God. God did give me the mission, the foundation scripture, the name of the group, and the name of our co-founder. I questioned God about the name he gave me to be the co-founder of this group because we knew of each other but never hung out. We were never what you would necessarily call "friends," but we were cordial. I reached out to her, and she gave God her YES, and now I am happy to call her my sister today.

The mission statement for Woman 2 Woman is as follows: "Our mission is to be women who not only exist but strive to be vessels of Christ who live intentionally. We are a group of imperfect women working together and using our God-given gifts to help others. Our purpose is to uplift, inspire, empower, encourage and motivate one another as well as sisters outside of our group regardless of race, religion, or creed to walk in your God-given purpose.

We are women of great integrity and dignity and do not promote or tolerate any form of degradation. We are advocates for togetherness and respect for self and others. We will be leaders by default. We are handpicked. We are women with different walks. "As Iron Sharpens Iron, so a friend sharpens a friend," Proverbs 27:17. "We are Woman 2 Woman (W2W)!"

Through gaining the courage to start this ministry, God made this scripture come alive… "I am far from oppression and will not live in fear." (Isaiah 54:14) If we want to fulfill our purpose and calling in life, we must know our identity in Christ. I now know I am fierce because I am a woman kept by God through trials and tribulations, through ups and downs, through mountains and valleys, through good times and bad times – THROUGH IT ALL GOD KEPT ME! I am fierce because God has given me the same power through the Holy Spirit that raised Jesus from the dead; it lives within me. I have permission to go boldly before the throne and pray our prayers. I can ask for what my heart desires. I have permission to join and agree with two or more believers, and he will answer. (Matthew 18:20) For where two or three are gathered together in my name, there am I in the midst of them.

I am fabulous because I am fearfully and wonderfully made (Psalm 139:14). I am a royal priesthood (1 Peter 2:9). I am above and not beneath (Deuteronomy 28:13). I am the lender and not the borrower. I am enough. I am more than a conqueror. I can do all things through Christ who strengthens me. I am fabulous because I now have the confidence to walk into a room with no validation or confirmation with full confidence in who I am and what I represent.

I am free because I set boundaries with people, even family. I stopped tolerating any kind of behavior and demanded respect from EVERYONE. I stopped allowing people to disturb my peace. When I see that a situation or circumstance is upsetting me, I step away from it, cool off, and approach it with a better attitude. I also stopped reacting to things and situations and started responding. There is a huge difference there. Reacting gives away your power to someone or something while responding gives you power and control of the situation. Reacting comes from a "bothered" or aggressive state of mind, while responding comes from a calm and peaceful state of mind. Reacting is unappealing to others and causes feelings of guilt and regret. Responding shows maturity and confidence. I learned 3 P's...Pause, Pray, Proceed.

I learned to quickly become aware of negative thoughts that came into my mind and started filling my mind with worship, even when I didn't feel like praying or listening to gospel music. I started recognizing when the enemy was inviting me to a pity party and started refusing to attend them. I stopped pretending to be ok and started seeking support. I learned that it is ok to not be ok. I could admit it and seek help. I started counseling, which unfortunately is frowned upon in the black community. I started taking self-care courses and started becoming more aware of my needs instead of always putting myself on the backburner so that I could care for everyone else. I started celebrating my accomplishments and wins, no matter how big or small. I started gratitude journaling, especially on those days when I felt down. I became determined to no longer remain stuck in the vicious roller coaster of emotions, one day up, then the next day down. Mind you, I do have down days; however, my approach to cope on those days is different now. I feel the feelings, and then I exercise my faith.

I recognized my limiting beliefs and changed them to limitless beliefs. I stopped comparing myself to others and started collaborating and congratulating other people's wins. I stopped allowing open doors to close and stopped missing opportunities that I prayed for, and started stepping out in faith. I stopped accepting self-condemnation and condemnation from others. I am free from the law of sin and death (Romans 8:2). I am free because I started liking and loving myself. I started respecting myself and thinking of myself in positive ways. I turned away from "stinking thinking." I am by no means perfect, but I am progressing. I am a forever student and continue to seek my worth and identity in Christ.

I realize that I must forever pursue my identity in Christ and affirm myself daily. I must remind myself that my identity is not defined by my past, is not defined by my titles, is not defined by my relationships, is not defined by my circumstances, is not defined by my feelings. In Christ is where I find my worth and my identity.

I try to make it a point daily to make a conscious effort to remind myself of who God says that I am. Affirm yourself today!

Affirmations

I maintain attitudes of gratitude and humility.

I am a child of God (1 John 4:4 You, dear children, are from God and have overcome them because the one who is in you is greater than the one who is in the world)

I have peace with God (John 14:27 Peace I leave with you; my peace I give you. I do not give to you as the world gives. Do not let your hearts be troubled and do not be afraid.)

I am the righteousness of God in Christ (2 Corinthians 5:21 God made him who had no sin to be sin for us so that in him we might become the righteousness of God.)

I am joyful (Psalm 16:11 You make known to me the path of life; you will fill me with joy in your presence, with eternal pleasures at your right hand.)

I am beautiful.

I am fearfully and wonderfully made (Psalm 139:14 I praise you because I am fearfully and wonderfully made; your works are wonderful, I know that full well.)

I am loved (John 16:27 No, the Father himself loves you because you have loved me and have believed that I came from God.)

I am blessed and a blessing to others.

I am the head and not the tail (Deuteronomy 28:13 The LORD will make you the head, not the tail. If you pay attention to the commands of the LORD your God that I give you this day and carefully follow them, you will always be at the top, never at the bottom.)

I am a royal priesthood (1 Peter 2:9 But you are a chosen people, a royal priesthood, a holy nation, God's special possession, that you may declare the praises of him who called you out of darkness into his marvelous light.)

I am confident.

I am seated with Christ in heavenly places (Ephesians 2:6 And God raised us up with Christ and seated us with him in the heavenly realms in Christ Jesus.)

God takes delight in me (Zephaniah 3:17 The LORD your God is with you, the Mighty Warrior who saves. He will take great delight in you; in his love, he will no longer rebuke you but will rejoice over you with singing.)

I am worthy and deserve to have a good life.

I have the mind of Christ (1 Corinthians 2:16 For, Who has known the mind of the Lord so as to instruct him? But we have the mind of Christ.)

I am renewed day by day.

I am fully known by God (1 Corinthians 13:12 For now, we see only a reflection as in a mirror; then we shall see face to face. Now I know in part; then I shall know fully, even as I am fully known.)

I am created in God's image (Genesis 1:27 So God created mankind in his own image, in the image of God he created them; male and female he created them.)

I am the salt of the earth and a light to the world.

I am free (John 8:36 So if the Son sets you free, you will be free indeed.)

Because I now know these truths, I can live empowered, fierce, fabulous, and free in Christ. Once you know your worth and identity in Christ, you can add tax.

I would like to share a prayer that I found for knowing your identity in Christ (www.crosswalk.com/faith/prayer/a-prayer-for-knowing-your-identity-in-christ.html).

A Prayer For Knowing Your Identity in Christ

Lord, I pray that You would unlock my heart that I might be fully alive to my true identity in You. Give me clear revelation to see myself the way You see me. Help me to stand in Your truth against all enemy attacks and guard my heart with all vigilance (Proverbs 4:23). Help me to identify the lies and reveal to me any places where I am chained to the past in a negative way. I repent of any lies of the past. [Name those lies and ask God to forgive you.] Teach me to hear Your voice and not believe the enemy's destructive lies about who I am. I thank You for my uniqueness and that I am made in Your image (Genesis 1:27). I want to understand and feel the deep things in Your heart for me (1 Corinthians 2:10-12).
I choose to believe the truth about how You see me. I thank You that I can hope in the future and believe in the good destiny that You have for me. You have a vision for my future. Help me to live a fruitful life now and overflow with Your love to others. Give me greater authority in my prayer life. I want to know You on a

deeper level, and I don't want anything to hinder my relationship with You.

I thank You that [Say your name instead of "I"]: I am Your child (John 1:12), I have been justified (Romans 5:1), I am Your friend (John 15:15), I belong to You (1 Corinthians 6:20), I am a member of Your body (1 Corinthians 12:27), I have been established, anointed, and sealed by You (2 Corinthians 1:21-22), I am a citizen of heaven (Philippians 3:20), I am blessed in the heavenly realms with every spiritual blessing (Ephesians 1:3), I am chosen before the creation of the world (Ephesians 1:4, 11), I am holy and blameless (Ephesians 1:4), I am forgiven (Ephesians 1:8; Colossians 1:14) I am adopted as Your child (Ephesians 1:5), I have purpose (Ephesians 1:9; 3:11), I have hope (Ephesians 1:12),I am included (Ephesians 1:13), I am an overcomer (1 John 4:4), I am protected (John 10:28), I am a new creation (2 Cor. 5:17), I am qualified to share in Your inheritance (Colossians 1:12), I am the righteousness of God (2 Corinthians 5:21), I am safe (1 John 5:18), I am part of Your Kingdom (Revelation 1:6), I can understand what Your will is (Ephesians 5:17), I have God's power (Ephesians 6:10), and I am victorious (1 Corinthians 15:57).

Thank You for this new identity I have in You. Help me to live out this truth in my life every day. In Jesus' name, amen."

-Jamaica Townsend

24.

Biography

Jamaica Townsend is a chaser after God's own heart first and foremost. She is a proud wife to Steven Townsend she is also the mother of 2 beautiful God-sent angels named Sanaiya and Zoe. Jamaica is the founder of a women's empowerment group based out of Springfield, TN called Woman 2 Woman (W2W). W2W provides a safe space for women to come together and release, pray and encourage one another to birth and walk in their God-given purpose. Jamaica is an intercessor and will pray on anyone's behalf. Jamaica is one of the Co-Authors of the Amazon # 1 Best Seller, SheEO Chronicles Volume 1 "20/20>2020", I am A Woman Empowered and Woman Empowered Anthology as well as the host of the "Matters of the Heart" Podcast. Jamaica is a public speaker and an aspiring Life Coach, motivational speaker, and entrepreneur in the arena of arts and crafts. She loves to encourage, pray for and inspire others to be who God created them to be.

IX

Valerie C. Thompson

25.

Dedication

I dedicate my chapter first to my three daughters and granddaughter!

- 1) My oldest daughter Jovan aka "JoJo" was born a leader! Every God given vision will manifest as it relates to entrepreneurship and multiple streams of income! Your creative and innovative Spirit will bless the masses! Keep going! I am extremely proud of you! You are built with much strength, courage, tenacity, compassion, and knowledge. There will be a performance! (Luke 1:45)

- 2) My bonus middle daughter DaKentra aka "Queen DK" is a bonified CEO! Keep your faith! Everything you touch will turn to gold! You were plated to prosper! Keep moving forward! You make my heart smile! Keep smiling and keep your heart open! God has so much more for you! I am thrilled about your NEXT! Every trial and tribulation came to build you from the inside out!

(James 1)

- 3) My youngest daughter Niara aka "Greater Purpose" is filled with wisdom! Thanking God, you will fulfil your God given assignment! You gifts and talents are evident, and God will continue to use you as you grow! Spread your wings and fly like the butterfly you are! You will succeed at whatever path you go down! You were chosen to win! I am grateful you are my daughter! Many are called, but few are chosen! (Matthew 22:14)

- 4) My one and only granddaughter Brielle aka "Strength" and trailblazer just like your mother! Continue to be persistent, animated, fearless, and determined! God will use you in a profound way! Your smile is contagious! Your conversation will open doors no man can shut! Your uniqueness speaks volumes! I am so blessed to be your grandmother! Angels will always protect you! Psalm 91-11-12

Second, to all women across the world – YOU ARE HERE FOR A REASON! YOU ARE HERE TO CREATE. LOVE, ACCERLATE, HEAL, and SOAR! The time is now! Look in the mirror and say, "I AM THAT ONE!" God makes no mistakes! Go get it! Do it! Go be it! YOU ARE IT! Your FAITH is leading the way! Hebrews 11:1

I am so excited for you! Thanking God, you move accordingly in your feminine and masculine energy to live your life on purpose! You are so significant and radiant! Someone is waiting for you! You are the answer to their prayers!

26.

Rise Lotus Flower

I am speaking to those who are listening and have committed to doing the work. God is speaking to those in this season who are waiting patiently on the Lord for the come-up because they have had experience in the setback! Do you hear me? According to Luke 12:35-48, Specifically scriptures 47-48, "And that servant, who knew his Lord's will and prepared not himself, neither did according to his will, shall be beaten with many stripes.48 But he that knew not and committed things worthy of stripes shall be beaten with few stripes. For unto whomsoever much is given, of him shall much be required; and to whom men have committed much, of him, they will ask the more." In your spare time, please read the whole chapter. I thank God the Holy Spirit will speak to you loud and clear. It behooves us to be in POSITION and PREPARING for the day God calls us to step our game up. We are not here to be mediocre!

I am sure you are thinking about what the above scripture has to do with Women Empowered – Fierce, Fabulous, and Free. I am glad you asked! You see, there is no way I could have accepted the invitation to be part of such a potent book if I did not believe I was a woman empowered. Empowered is defined as – having the knowledge, confidence, means, or ability to do things or make decisions for oneself; make (someone) stronger and more confident, especially in controlling their life and claiming their rights.

Prefix (EM) is defined as – "put in or into, bring to a certain state,"

Power – possession of control, authority, or influence over others; the ability to move things without resistance.

Back to Luke 12:47-48, If I were not obedient to the Word of God over my life, I would not have taken the initiative (Holy Spirit led) to prepare myself over the years (doing the internal work of healing despite the temporary situations and circumstances I have faced over the years). I would have immediately Self-Sabotaged when the visionary asked me to be a part of this movement. It becomes our obligation to believe who God already calls us from the beginning. Jeremiah 1:5 states, "Before I formed you in your mother's womb, I thought of you and set you apart to prophesy to the nations." Wait a minute, Lord, you are telling me you thought about little ole me, my characteristics, my temperament, my emotions, my trauma, my drama, and everything in between? You knew from the beginning, despite my issues, that I was Fierce, Fabulous, & Free? The moral of this story is to stay ready, so you do not have to get ready! Once you know WHO and WHOSE you are, you will prepare yourself to show up when God calls.

An empowered woman knows she was created to shift the atmosphere! She knows she is a world changer. She knows she is called to speak life. She understands the calling on her life. She believes she can and will. She trusts the Spirit (Holy Spirit), which guides her into all truth and understanding. She is esteemed. She knows her worth. She is Fierce, Fabulous, and Free!

Fierce – having or expressing bold confidence or style.

When Lady Fierce shows up in our lives, we believe in ourselves and the power of the Holy Spirit to guide us into all truth and understanding. Embracing Lady Fierce triggers, us to ask for what we want and honestly believe we will receive it. It whispers in our ears to apply for a position we are not qualified for. Lady Fierce walks with us and reminds us to walk this journey out unapologetically. Lady Fierce knows it is conducive to connect and collaborate with other phenomenal women to create communities and platforms which support healing, encouragement, and inspiration for one another.

Fabulous – extraordinary, especially extraordinarily large; going beyond what is usual, regular, or customary.

Let me tell you a little bit about walking with Sister Fabulous. She pulls you out of places no longer serving you. She never allows you to go along to get along. She speaks to you loud and clear and says, "Get out here!" She pushes you into purpose where you meet leaders, creators, visionaries, queens, and boss ladies. She propels you to accept the calling, mantle, and assignment over your life. She invigorates you to live your best life. Sister Fabulous will no longer allow you to rent space to negativity, procrastination, stagnation, and excuses. She is not afraid to raise the rent and kick the tenants out! She knows her worth and will not compromise for anyone or anything.

Free – not under the control or in the power of another; able to act or be done as one wishes; not or no longer confined or imprisoned; release from captivity, confinement, or slavery.

Ladies, mindset is everything! We can be released from a situation or circumstance physically; however, mentally stay imprisoned. Have you ever thought about people who spend years in prison? Wherein the prison gates are more like a revolving door. When the prisoner is released, he/she usually returns to prison because it is a familiar place physically, as well as mentally. As it relates to recidivism, the statistics in California are around 50%. (https://worldpopulationreview.com/state-rankings/recidivism-rates-by-state) It is essential to do the necessary work from the inside out to recognize FREEDOM and take the steps required to walk in it.

When we accept Queen Free into our lives, we are free to create the life we desire to live. Queen Free appears when we take the responsibility to do the healing work top to bottom, side to side, and inward to outward. Queen Free shares her viewpoints with a mind no longer imprisoned. This mind has the capacity to stretch her thoughts and create supernatural experiences. Thus, Queen Free has a new taste and a new smell; it is a whole vibe!

Queen Free allows us to visualize territory we have never chartered physically; however, we have touched spiritually. Queen Free draws us to tap into creativity, imagination, and expansion on every level. Queen Free spreads her wings every chance she gets because she knows she will excel at everything she puts her heart and mind to!

Backend –

I grew up in the outskirts of San Francisco, CA., in a middle-class neighborhood full of culture and hard-working young families in the 70s and 80s. Our family home was a two-story, three bedroom/1 bath, two-car garage house. Both of my parents worked decent jobs. My father worked as a truck driver for the post office, and my mother usually worked as a cashier somewhere. Originally from Montgomery, AL., my father graduated from high school and went to the Air Force. On the other hand, my mother, originally from Houston, TX., did not graduate from high school. She dropped out in the 11th grade, got married to my father, and they had their first child, my brother in 1969. I was born in 1972, I AM THAT ONE!.

I cannot say I knew anything about embracing the term fierce, fabulous, or free growing up in my household. Do not even bring up the word empowerment. I did not know it then as a child because I only knew what I knew. I know my parents loved my brother and I; however, I do not think they understood love as it relates to marriage. You see, some of my earliest recollections are my parents arguing and fighting. Unbeknownst to me, I had no clue how being smack dab in the middle of their toxic marriage would shape and mold me as a teenager and young lady. There is no way I could have clothed myself in empowerment and freedom, let alone embrace who God predestined me to be from the very beginning. God already Declared and Decreed I was Fabulous and Fierce. Think about it, if I (we) were created in the image of God as according to Genesis 1:27-28 –

God spoke: "Let us make human beings in our image, make them

reflecting our nature

So they can be responsible for the fish in the sea,

the birds in the air, the cattle,

And, yes, Earth itself,

and every animal that moves on the face of Earth."

God created human beings;

he created them godlike,

Reflecting God's nature.

He created them male and female.

God blessed them:

"Prosper! Reproduce! Fill Earth! Take charge!

Be responsible for fish in the sea and birds in the air,

for every living thing that moves on the face of Earth."

No matter what we come from as it relates to the hardships or challenges, we face, we must know without any doubt we are built to last! The temporary situations and circumstances come to distract us. Thus, if we lean into God, we know that our character is being shaped for the greater. Character building is required to do the will of God. God is looking for women who know what it means to endure, stand the test of time, press forward, impact, and keep the momentum while in the game of life.

This level does not allow self-doubt, pity, unsettled emotions, or limiting beliefs to get on the plane with you traveling to your next destination.

The vision

Habakkuk 2:2-3

And then God answered: "Write this.

Write what you see.

Write it out in big block letters

so that it can be read on the run.

This vision message is a witness

pointing to what's coming.

It aches for the coming—it can hardly wait!

And it doesn't lie.

If it seems slow in coming, wait.

It's on its way. It will come right on time.

Jeremiah 29:11 – I will bless you with a future filled with hope—a future of success, not of suffering

What has God called you to do? Who has God called you to help?

What group of people are you called to lead out of a dark and desolate place? It is crucial as an empowered woman to recognize this life does not belong to you. This life belongs to our creator, aka GOD! As a reminder, God thought of you from the very beginning and had something special only you could do for the people you are specifically designated to support on this journey.

When was the last time you sat down and checked in with God to see if you were on the right track? When was the last time you asked God to reveal himself to you in detail about a comprehensive outline or blueprint for your life, aka purpose? The vision God wants to share with you is massive because you are called to the masses. The vision God has for you requires you to believe from a place of ENORMOUS faith! The vision God will download requires you to open your mind to community, connection, and collaboration for the MAGNANIMOUS territory you are called to possess.

Deuteronomy 11:10-12 The land you are entering to take up ownership is not like Egypt, the land you left, where you had to plant your own seed and water it yourselves as in a vegetable garden. But the land you are about to cross the river and take for your own is a land of mountains and valleys; it drinks water that rains from the sky. It is a land that God, your God, personally tends—he is the gardener—he alone keeps his eye on it all year long.

Yes, the revelation God will share may intimidate you initially; however, that is a good thing. Do not run from it; embrace it as God will provide provision for the vision. God is Jehovah Jireh! Thank God for speaking to you through dreams and spiritual visualization.

Own Your Truth and Rise

The truth is, you and I are here today to bless the masses through our various gifts and talents. God specifically chose you and me to bring joy to people who are downtrodden and hopeless. We were created to build facilities for the homeless, feed and clothe the disadvantaged, build schools in low-income communities, live as missionaries overseas, be the light in this dark world, support others as they heal, create programs to assist people who have been abused, become an author and share your story to encourage someone else, become a public speaker and uplift, someone, through your transparency, become a singer and bless others by the presence of peace in your voice...the list goes on and on.

Tools to help you become Fierce, Fabulous, and Free!

- Prophesy over your life daily (Speak well of your life daily. Speak well of your body. Focus on all the great aspects about you.)
- Take time daily for you (Do something kind for yourself daily)
- Seek God for yourself daily (thirty minutes to an hour or more if you have the time)
- Pray (Thank God for EVERYTHING & EVERYONE)
- Meditate (While sitting with your thoughts, pay attention to what you hear. God is giving you strategic plans)
- Journal (Journal your thoughts. What has the Holy Spirit shared with you?)
- Goals (Write down goals for the day, week, month, year – 5 years)
- Visualization (Practice seeing spiritually what you do not see physically. You must see yourself living the life you deserve and desire)
- Do not be afraid to step out of comfort! Stepping out of comfort allows you to get uncomfortable and walk-through new doors.

- Never stop dreaming and believing!
- If you have childhood trauma – Do the necessary work to REVEAL, DEAL, & HEAL!

Philippians 4:13 – I can do all things through [a]Christ who strengthens me.

God has a mighty work for you to do while you are here for a limited time only.

Walk-in all POWER, AUTHORITY & DOMINION

I release the supernatural favor of EXPANSION, MULTIPLICATION, INCREASE, DIVINE ENCOUNTERS, MULTILEVEL LUCRATIVE BUSINESSES, KINGDOM MARRIAGES, KINGDOM RELATIONSHIPS & MANIFESTATION! You are walking in a season of double for your trouble. You are basking in a season of prophetic impartation. You shall open your mouth and DECLARE & DECREE a thing, and it will be established (Job 22:28). Every single prayer that comes forth from your mouth shall accomplish what you have placed in the atmosphere, according to (Isaiah 55:11). I declare and decree an Issachar Anointing over your life! Get ready for the impossible. Receive the suddenly and believe your words move mountains, heal the sick, give hope to the hopeless, and shift the atmosphere. (John 14:12)

However, as it is written: "What no eye has seen, what no ear has heard, and what no human mind has conceived" — the things God has prepared for those who love him—

(1 Corinthians 2:9)

1 If you listen obediently to the Voice of God, your God, and heartily obey all his commandments that I command you today,

God, your God, will place you on high, high above all the nations of the world.

2 All these blessings will come down on you and spread out beyond you because you have responded to the Voice of God, your God:

3 God's blessing inside the city, God's blessing in the country.

4 God's blessing on your children, the crops of your land, the young of your livestock, the calves of your herds, the lambs of your flocks.

5 God's blessing on your basket and bread bowl.

6 God's blessing in your coming in, God's blessing in your going out.

7 God will defeat your enemies who attack you. They will come at you on one road and run away on seven roads.

8 God will order a blessing on your barns and workplaces; he will bless you in the land that God, your God, is giving you.

9 God will form you as a people holy to him, just as he promised you, if you keep the commandments of God, your God, and live the way he has shown you.

10 All the peoples on Earth will see you living under the Name of God and hold you in respectful awe.

11 God will lavish you with good things: children from your womb, offspring from your animals, and crops from your land, the land that God promised your ancestors that he would give you.

12 God will throw open the doors of his sky vaults and pour rain on your land on schedule and bless the work you take in hand. You

will lend to many nations, but you yourself will not have to take out a loan.

13 God will make you the head, not the tail; you will always be the top dog, never the bottom dog, as you obediently listen to and diligently keep the commands of God, your God, that I am commanding you today.

Deuteronomy 28:1-13

Empowered – Fierce, Fabulous & Free

You are fierce – Never intimidated or duplicated!

You are fabulous. They say you do too much; you say I do not do enough!

You are free. God clipped your wings last season to equip you for a reason this season. It is time to take flight. Your whole life is about to be unrecognizable.

It ain't over!

27.

Biography

Life does not always paint a picture clear enough for one to understand.

Helping to bring clients both a brush and a new lens on life, Valerie Thompson was created to encourage, inspire, and uplift women, one at a time.

Valerie C. Thompson is a multi-faceted entrepreneur, author, speaker, advocate, empowerment, and spiritual Coach; with a heart for women who have experienced childhood trauma from the shackles of domestic violence. Unresolved childhood trauma turns into adult drama if healing does not take place.

Valerie is the founder of Own Your Truth & Rise Coaching/Consulting wherein she provides clients with the support needed to take ownership of their healing, and to provide them with various strategies, so that they can operate *in purpose, on purpose, for God's huge purpose.* Valerie helps her clients to recognize their temporary circumstance as a catalyst for the creation of a new life. Valerie also works as a part-time Social Worker.

Using her gifts to inspire, Valerie has created several avenues to service clientele. She is the founder of platforms; Host of Own Your Truth (Conversations about Domestic Violence) on Facebook Live (for the month of October), and visionary of The Woman the Gifts; by which, women share entrepreneurship strategies, and stories of how they delegate their gifts in the world. She also hosts a podcast titled Own Your Truth and Rise!

Valerie is also the author of e-book, Your *Soul is Free – Encouragement from A to Z, Co*-author *of Before the Vows Break: Tales of Triumph, co-author of best-selling book Finally Free, co-author of Women Who Pray and co-author for best seller Reinvented to Rise and Visionary over From Trauma & Drama to Truth scheduled to be released at the end of 2021!*

Valerie has a love for people and helps others to paint a new picture of themselves, through the power of understanding that we all can create the life we desire to live by being intentional about changing our thoughts, visualization, and action.

Valerie's life is a true reminder that we are all here to impact the world in a profound way, and that the *journey of healing amplifies our impact.*

Valerie is a mother of four gifted and talented children and a grandmother of phenomenal twins!

Valerie C. Thompson – Vessel for God!

X
P' Angela Jones

28.

Dedication

I want to thank my Mom and all the women in my life that showed me that FIERCE, FABULOUS, and FREE was not a lifestyle but a mindset. Thank you, Darryl Jones, for pushing me to tell my story. I dedicate this book to my daughters that they would walk in the legacy of the power of a sound mind.

29.

Fierce Fabulous & Free: A Mindset

Personal development is a great equalizer. You can grow from good to great at any stage in your life. The playing field of self-improvement is leveled and here's why:

- Anyone can change. Change is not reserved for the strongest or most tenacious.
- Everyone can level up. You can decide at any given time that you're going higher.
- You can start from anywhere and go up! The greatest truth about hitting rock bottom is that you can only go up from there!

There is only one requirement needed to reach the next-level living, and it's a resource that everyone on earth has access to—the right mindset.

Growing up, I remember seeing billboards, watching commercials, and hearing my grandmother say to me, "P'Angela, a mind is a terrible thing to waste." This was a popular campaign that was developed to keep young black kids in the 70s and 80's off drugs. It was the Ad Council's hope that we would stay out of the streets and onto the path to college, higher education, and a greater lifestyle than the ones with which we were accustomed.

Yet, I would think to myself, "I'm not just pretty-I'm smart! Grandmother, why would you think I'm not using all of my brain?" It's not that our grandparents thought we weren't using our brains; our wiser elders were concerned about our mindsets. Most of us would say our minds are operating on full cylinders. We are cognitive thinking and discerning people; we use rationale and deductive reasoning.

A mindset, however, is much different than just thinking in general. Your mindset is how you think. The definition of mindset consists of cultivating "an established set of attitudes held about yourself." To be honest, a mindset is never wasting away; it has the room to consistently grow, develop and adapt to become better. It's all about the attitudes you hold.

Are you ready to hold a new mindset? New mindsets are built with new language. Expanding your vocabulary and giving language to your inner hopes, dreams, and desires is how you unlock a fresh mindset.

The FIERCE FABULOUS AND FREE Mindset

FIERCE

Outdated definition: having or displaying an intense or ferocious aggressiveness.

Passionate definition: A word used to describe something that is out of the box, non-traditional, and dynamic. Passionate, joyful, and positive! Fierce means to demand excellence. Fierce is about inclusivity, honesty, authenticity.

The Mindset shift: What's your position on being fierce? We all want to think out of the box but are we living outside the box? As women who live in this pseudo-misogynistic society, I know we have to be intent on our desire to become the women GOD created us to be. We also must have an intense desire for greater and better within our souls. Ferocity is beautiful! Don't be ashamed; we are well-crafted storms designed to shake up the norms of society, and we are aggressive to create, build and protect our families.

FREE:

Outdated definition: The quality or state of being free, not a slave.

Passionate definition: Able to act at will, not under compulsion or restraint. Having personal rights or liberty; not enslaved or confined, fully accepted and approved.

The Mindset Shift: I am free to create, build, deliver, and be. There is nothing to hold me back, hold me down, or enslave me except for me. My mind is sound, powerful, creative, strong, and free. My heart is receptive, unclogged, softened, loving, and free. My body isn't bound, my soul isn't captive, my voice is heard, and I am free.

FABULOUS:

Outdated definition: extraordinary, especially extraordinarily large.

Passionate definition: Everything you always wanted maturating in your life. Opulent, over-the-top, exquisite, and memorable.

The Mindset Shift: I am not only fabulous in life, but I am fabulous in thought. My self-talk is outstanding, my self-image powerful, my sights are set on only things above. I'm high-minded and proud of it because my thoughts have no business being low.

You see, Fierce Fabulous and Free is a mindset. Becoming fierce, becoming strong, becoming focused on your passion – that's a mindset. Being fabulous, being beautiful, being overwhelmingly confident – that's a mindset. Being free, being liberated, being convicted with who you are, the way you are, that starts all in the mind as well. I am excited to be a part of this project because I understand that anyone, at any time, can be fierce, fabulous, and free if you train your mind. Listen, do it for yourself this season. Be a part of this movement. Be fierce, be fabulous, be free – it starts with YOU!

30.

Biography

Mrs. P'Angela Jones is a Certified Professional Life Coach whose expertise is Passion Coaching; helping women, entrepreneurs and couples uncover or discover their passion. She believes all relationships deserve a success strategy so she's made helping women cultivate a healthy life her personal passion. She is skilled at helping women create their personal and family brands through character development. She is an author, ordained elder, contributing writer for iShine magazine, a marriage education advocate, and an Exclusive Event Host. She is the Chaplain and Director of SheEO C.A.R.E.S., the faith and service department of the nationally recognized women's organization, The SheEO District. She is also an African American drink maker and crafts uniquely flavored mimosas at her mobile bar, Morning Do Mimosa. She lives a full and beautiful life with her husband and six children in North Atlanta, Ga. You can stay connected to her through her website TheMorningDo.org and by connecting her with women who need a life makeover OR passing her name along to event planners and conference developers!

XI

Carnesha Stanton

31.

Dedication

To every little girl that thinks she is not worthy. Your goals are possible if YOU believe in yourself.

32.

Freedom From The Past!

A past is something that everyone has, and we sometimes try to do our very best to forget certain parts of the past. Of course, some try to forget about their past because of the drama it may have caused, and then there or some who even try to deny it due to shame. I have done both. Then I have those memories that are so precious to me that I never want to forget them.

My past, however, is what has caused me to grow into the beautiful, bold, courageous, amazing, talented woman I am today. I am the product of an inner-city upbringing where both of my parents were addicts. I am not sure of my mother's actual addiction, but it had something to do with a white powder she sniffed through her nose. I later found out my father was addicted to heroin and eventually became an alcoholic. He simply traded one addiction for another.

As far as I can remember, my mother was a beautiful person who had many issues, including a drug addiction of her own. This caused my sister and I to always bounce between living with her and our aunt. I can recall an instance during the time of living with my mom when I woke up in the middle of the night to find that my mother had left my sister and me in the house by ourselves. Afraid and unsure of what was happening, I woke up my baby sister to look for her. We lived in an inner-city project, "Cabrini Green," so after leaving the building and not sure where to go exactly, I went to across the street to the local police department and explained I didn't know where my mom was, and I was scared.

I had to only be about five or six years old at this time, so the police asked me all of the preliminary information. I answered every question to the best of my ability. I explained that my great-grandmother lived close by and I could take my sister there. I'm not sure of the exact details, but one of the officers recognized me and stated they knew my family. Not long after that, my grandmother walked into the police station to claim us both. I was excited to see a familiar face but again afraid because I still didn't know where my mother was.

My grandmother was ill; she actually left the hospital to come to see about us, so we were sent to my aunt's house again for a few days. Finally, my mother came back around, and back into her care we went. Things seemed to be back on track for a while, or at least they appeared to be. This time my sister woke up looking for our mom. Unable to find her, she woke me up to help her look, and like before, my mother was gone. I got my sister dressed so we could go looking for her. I found a key hanging on the closet door in the hallway. I hoped it was to the door, so I could lock it behind us (the first time I'd left the door unlocked but was sure to close it). The key fit, so I grabbed my baby sisters' hand, and we walked the three flights down the stairway. I bypassed the police station this time, heading straight to a friend of my mother's.

I could see the lights were on from outside, but I was afraid of this building. I thought if I stood downstairs and yelled up to the window, my mother would hear my voice and come on out. Well, I did just that; however, no one showed up. I stood outside for a while, yelling her name periodically, then a familiar face walked up. It was my father. I started crying, explaining the situation. Upset, he began to shout my mother's name, and after a few minutes, she came walking out of the building at a fast pace. She and my father exchanged words with one another. I'm not exactly sure what was said, but she grabbed both my sister and my hands and briskly walked us back to our apartment.

Once we arrived, I began to cry hysterically, apologizing to her for leaving the house. I explained my sister was scared, which made me scared, so we only wanted to find her. She hugged me tightly and told me it was okay, stating she left the key for me and that I was now a big girl; the key was mine. She thanked me for not going to the police station this time. I never found out why she didn't answer me when I called her name, but I was excited that I wasn't in trouble. I fell back to sleep. After all, I was now a big girl with a key to the house.

Situations like these continued to take place until the night of the fire. Someone threw a homemade grenade into my bedroom window – starting a fire that spread through the entire apartment. My sister and I were spending the night with family members, so we weren't home. After we lost everything in the fire, we had to move in with my grandmother. A few months later, my mother decided it was best for my sister and I to move in with my aunt permanently; this was November of 1989.

The following February, at the age of 28 years young, she passed away from this life two weeks after her birthday. The cause of death was a heart attack as a result of pneumonia. I was only nine years old at the time. Since we already lived with my aunt, she decided to adopt my sister and I, ensuring we would no longer have a hard life.

I admit that life wasn't hard, but it wasn't particularly easy either. She did her best if you asked me; after all, she had three children of her own and still took us in. The lifestyle change we experienced was good for the most part. We no longer had to live in the projects but were now residents of a five-bedroom house. Drugs were no longer part of my life. My aunt barely drank a beer in our presence; she'd quit smoking and never had a man over (at least while we were home). After my mom's death, the only men that were consistent in my life were my grandfather and our new Pastor (who I later began to call my dad). Being that neither resided in the home with me, there were still things I yearned for as a young lady. I was never taught how a man should treat and love a woman. The real life examples that were before me showed me how to be a bitter black woman. Yes, I learned every cliché and thought they were the only way.

My biological father relinquished all legal rights to me when I was only ten years old. I later found out I was present when this occurred, but neither of us knew. I didn't see or talk to him for six years after that day. My Aunt told me that he didn't love me or want me, and if he had, I would be living with him and not her. My heart began to harden towards the man I looked so much like. I felt abandoned by my only living parent and thought the words were true because each year, after signing over his rights, he fathered another child. This longing for love led me down a road of heartache and pain that I once thought I would never recover from.

I met my ex-husband when I was 18 years old, and he was 29 years old. We started off as coworkers first. I was not interested in this man at all. He pursued me until I had a change of heart. During the course of the 8-year relationship I maintained with him, I found myself so low I thought I would never rise from the hole I allowed him to dig for me. I will never forget the day he decided to take me as his own. After working at a car dealership for about three months, I arrived at work dressed in a gray form-fitting sweater dress; it was a cool September night in Illinois. As I walked down the street and passed the smaller lot where he primarily worked, I heard a voice call my name. Baffled, I turned around and answered. Seeing him walk briskly towards me, I slowed my speedy walk, allowing him to catch up. My life would never be the same from that moment as this is the day he decided his 29-year-old self wanted a relationship with an 18-year old girl.

Yes, I identified myself as a girl because I see how immature I was even to allow myself to enter such a toxic relationship. However, had you asked me my status at that time, I would have told you I was a grown woman because I was doing grown woman things, working two jobs, and taking care of myself. Yet that was truly not the case. Needless to say, I fell for every word and began to love the man that supposedly loved me from the first day he'd ever seen me. Every day after work, he would take me back to his place and make love to my young body as if I was as fully grown as I perceived to be. Some nights he would take me home; other nights, I would stay over. He treated me like a queen, taking me to expensive restaurants and praising me for my behavior of never asking questions, even when the red flags were ever so present.

A few months into this fairytale relationship, I found out I was pregnant. I'll never forget the day I told him the news. After all, he stated I would be the mother of his first son. Well, things didn't go as I planned. His reaction was cold, and the words he spoke would burn a hole in my heart. "Well, maybe you should have an abortion, then we can try again because there is no way that is my child!" Devasted by his reaction, I actually contemplated the idea because I loved him so much, and the love he showed me prior to this day was absolutely amazing. However, after consideration and not properly healing from making that same decision the year prior, I decided to move forward with the pregnancy without the assistance of the man that I loved and thought loved me the same.

After giving birth to my first-born son, I contacted him to advise of this new bundle of joy. As expected, he was extremely cold and didn't care. However, three days after my release, he called and asked if he could see the baby that couldn't possibly be his. I obliged and allowed for the introduction because I was confident that his heart would change once he laid eyes on our son. Needless to say, I was correct; he did just that. This man was so excited to finally have a son that he began making life changes and purchasing his first property to allow for residual income for his children. He wanted to secure my son's future, or so I thought. This is where things took a turn for the worse in my life. I was only 19 years old when I gave birth to my son. Believing every word this man told me, I moved out of my family home to start a life with him.

I would love this man so much that he will have no choice but to keep his promises of making me his wife. I wasn't prepared for the manipulation and emotional abuse that I set myself up to endure. See, he felt as if I trapped him into becoming a family man after he'd been a bachelor for so long, yet it was what he said he wanted. But nothing I had ever endured prior to this relationship could have prepared me for the pain I experienced with this man.

I can't say I didn't know he could be so mean because, during my pregnancy, we continued to work together for a short time. He flaunted women in my face on those days he ignored me. During our time of living together, different women would stop by our home, and he would walk outside to greet them. Some left gifts at the door thanking him for their time together, just like the beginning of our relationship. I turned my head and looked the other way.

I found myself pregnant again and afraid of his reaction (because of the previous trauma). I was scared to tell him, but I suffered through what I thought would be a painful conversation. He was more accepting of it but suggested I have an abortion because our son was so young. Well, I agreed, only to find out a few weeks later that he fathered another baby with one of the women he already had a daughter with. I was heartbroken but still in love.

I moved out of the home we shared in an attempt to get my thoughts together, but I was not willing to leave him alone completely. This cycle of pregnancy and abortions continued for years. See, his goal, in my opinion, was to keep me barefoot and pregnant; however, the issue was he was doing this with someone else as well. Over the course of our relationship, I had four abortions, one when I was as far as five months pregnant. I can't put all of the blame on him because I later realized these were also choices of my own making. I allowed this man access to my body without protection. I was the one who went to the clinic to simply discard a pregnancy as if it was actual birth control. It was the very last abortion that I had, where the doctor looked me sternly in the face and explained to me this was not okay. She educated me on how I damaged my body even more each time I underwent an abortion.

After this last procedure, my body went through changes. I bled longer than normally expected, passing very large blood clots. I had to undergo numerous tests as the doctors thought I possibly had a form of cancer, which scared me.

Thank God I was cancer-free; I only had the case of stupidity for a man that clearly did not love me. However, that didn't stop me from wanting him even more. I began praying to God to change his heart so that he could be the man of my dreams. I asked that God allow him to love me only so that we could be a happy family. I was willing to accept all of his children, even the two he had during the relationship. My prayer was so sincere that I asked God to please show me if this man was for me. Instantly my body became wretched with fever, I was shivering horribly, and the only other person with me was my son. I called my "man" and asked that he please come take me to the hospital, because I couldn't drive and needed someone to get our son. His response confirmed the question I'd asked in my prayer, "No, I'm not coming. Call the ambulance and someone in your family to get the baby. I'm busy," and he hung the phone up, no longer answering it afterward. I was devastated.

See, these acts alone made me too ashamed to tell my story. I felt people would criticize me for being so vulnerable, or they would think less of me if they only knew what I've done or what I've gone through. But I realized that everyone has a past; some try to run from it and forget it, while some never embrace it. So yes, after those horrible experiences, my lesson still was not learned. I had my moments of empowerment, where I left, but I always went back. I even agreed to become his wife.

During that last breakup, things were different. He called every day and even went as far as to cry and threaten to commit suicide. I eventually gave in to his threats, not wanting to be responsible for his death (he was lying only to get me back). I decided it would be okay to entertain conversations with him. I would stay on the phone with him all night just to make sure he was okay, getting nervous during the daytime when he didn't answer the phone. I played right into his manipulation antics that I actually laugh at now.

The day he asked me to marry him was a day of excitement and nerves. He asked me to meet him at a local shopping mall as he needed to show me something. Without hesitation, I drove to the mall to meet him. Upon my arrival, he was the ultimate gentleman opening my door and wanting to walk hand in hand inside. I was too afraid to ask what store we were heading to or what he needed to pick up. He grabbed my hand and led me to the jewelry store (anxiety building, I was thinking he was having me pick out something for the woman he'd been cheating on me with). We walked up to the counter, and the young lady was surprised and asked, "Is this her" with the biggest smile I'd ever seen. He replied, "Yes, this is her." The young lady stated I was absolutely beautiful and so lucky. I had no idea what she was speaking of.

He interrupted my thoughts and said, "Hey, look at this case. Which of these rings do you want?" Shocked, I pointed to the 2-carat diamond ring with round stones along the side. The ring sat in white gold and just sparkled. I said, "That one right there." The sales lady gasped loudly and asked, "HOW?" Still not aware of what was going on, he nodded to her, and she took the ring out of the case. Still shocked, I finally asked what was going on here. The sales lady answered me and explained he'd just paid for that exact ring and how he couldn't stop talking about me and how much he loved me. She asked if the ring was to be placed on my finger. He stopped her and stated, "No, please put it in the box. I'll give it to her later."

This made me upset and confused. How could he purchase the ring of my dreams and tell this lady how much he loved me, then not give it to me? My mind started racing again, and the thoughts of him making me pick out a gift for the other woman came back. He stopped me mid-thought as we approached the escalator and asked if I would marry him. Not thinking, my dumb self blurted out yes, and he placed the ring on my finger. We were married two weeks later.

The marriage itself lasted three years total but only about five months with the two of us living together. Two months into the marriage, the financial bind he was in as a result of losing his job prior to our shotgun marriage, was revealed. Vehicles were repossessed, credit card balances were out of control, and the mortgage started to fall behind. And it all became my fault, as he reminded me that my leaving him sent him into a depression. It was my fault that his relationship with one of the mothers of his daughters failed. It was all my fault, and now he resented me and hated the day I ever entered his life. What a blow! I was broken by his words and actions, knowing I prayed for this man, had abortions for this man, and was outcasted by some family members for this man.

I had to consider the part I played and take responsibility for it. Yes, it was my fault to allow a man to take advantage of me so young. Yes, it was my fault for allowing him to continue impregnating me and have abortions as if they were birth control. Yes, it was my fault to continue to stick by his side after he had two children on me, one only six months younger than our son. Yes, it was my fault for staying. So, since all of this was my fault, I decided to exit stage left and move on with my life. I wanted out of that toxic marriage as this was not my vision of how it should be. Of course, he threatened me, stating he'd get custody of our son as he would explain to the judge how much of an unfit mother I am. He would use my own medical records against me and tell them to check for the scar tissue because I had so many abortions.

This shook me, but I refused to allow it to hold me down. I had to remember I was a survivor; I'd survive the death of my mother and those nights she left my sister and I alone. I survived the deaths of close loved ones, which showed me I was strong enough to fight. I just needed to heal from my past. And in order to do that, I needed to embrace my past choices and process each incident as if it was a step in a staircase. I know that it's possible to fall down or even trip up or down a stair, but the most important thing to remember is even when you fall, you can always get back up.

So, I tackled that staircase of my life, taking one step at a time, so even during those times that I fell, there was always room for me to get up and keep climbing. I began looking to the hills from where my help came from and knew that all my help came from the Lord alone.

That first marriage taught me a lesson of knowing I deserved so much more. I am worthy of true love and would one day find it. However, I had to allow God to send me the man in whom He wanted me to be a helpmate too. And He did just that. I am now remarried to a man that genuinely honors me and understands Proverbs 18:22 "He who finds a wife finds a good thing and obtains favor from the Lord." I've learned marriage is not necessarily easy, but it is also not hard as long as you put in the work.

I thank God for my journey. I fought those battles that were meant to destroy me but actually made me aware of the fact that I am FIERCE! I endured the fire along the way, but I did not smell like smoke. I do not look like what I've been through; this made me realize just how FABULOUS I am. I gave my life over to God. By the saving grace of his son Jesus and the fact that my past was cast into the sea of forgetfulness, I know that I am indeed FREE!

33.

Biography

I am Evangelist Carnesha Stanton, ordained in March 2009 at New St. Peters M.B.C. Deliverance in Chicago Illinois.

Having a servant's heart and compassion for youth, I served as Youth Pastor of a children's ministry for five years. Mentoring children between the ages of 5-16 years old, building lasting relationships and providing a level of security all while empowering them for the future.

With a passion for cooking since the age of nine, and loving to entertain, I began a small business "Pretty Tastee Treats" providing catering needs for small church meetings and baked goods to the public. My specialty is "banana pudding and peach cobbler."

XII

Natashah Khan

34.

Dedication

I dedicate this book first and foremost to GOD and my two beautiful daughters Isabella Jasmine James and Haley Brianna James. GOD gifted me with these two beautiful, intelligent, talented women who helped me survive my past and continue to be my inspiration for living every day. Thank you for always being there for me, supporting my dreams and being my number one fans. I pray that my past experiences will inspire you to have the COURAGE to speak up, walk in FAITH, always knowing and trusting that GOD will always be there to help you overcome any obstacle and to LOVE yourself and others UNCONDITIONALLY!!

I also dedicate this to those sick and suffering, struggling with mental health issues and or substance abuse issues, know that there is HOPE!

To All of the AMAZING women GOD allowed me to cross paths with along the way of my journey, you know who you are, there are just too many to mention that have been inspirational, empowering and supportive; but here are just a few that have remained constant in my life and love me for who I am – Lee Vitaliano, Melissa Bryan, Jessica Berry, Sarah Broughton and Dr. Nicole Ozunion. Special Thank You to a beautiful angel here on earth- Nefretiri Mc Griff, I would not be allotted this opportunity to have my story be shared with so many, if it wasn't for you. Thank You for always believing in me and being such a beautiful gift in my life.

Finally, to my Birth Family- Thank You for giving me life and always pushing me to be greater!

To My Online Families (Support Group Members) Thank You for Your Support & Encouragement that strengthened my faith to step out and be Fierce, Fabulous and Free!

35.

Free!!

What Does It Mean to Be Fierce, Fabulous, and Free?

I am FREE from the bondage of unhealthy relationships, pursuit of money, dissatisfying jobs, and emotional pain and suffering I endured at the hands of someone else's poor behaviors or decision-making. **I am FIERCE** today because GOD showed me mercy, grace, and forgiveness. He taught me how to love myself unconditionally, despite all the years of my voice being silenced due to bullying, being discriminated against, unresolved trauma, grief, and loss, and negative self-beliefs such as but not limited to "my opinion doesn't matter," "I am not of value," "I am not worthy of anything good," and "I am not lovable." My walk and relationship with GOD have set me free, strengthened me mentally, emotionally, and spiritually, and reminded me that I have a voice. It is meant to be heard despite what others may think or say. **I am FABULOUS** because **I get** to be unapologetically me. I love myself and others unconditionally as GOD loves me, and I live life today free from being held captive mentally and emotionally. I am free to speak my truth and not let fear, guilt/shame, or negative opinions of others continue to silence me. I am finally free to be the woman GOD has called me to be and live my purpose-driven life!

Where it all Began!

I must take you back to the beginning of where life began. I was born and raised in the Caribbean islands of Trinidad and Tobago by both my parents. My older sister and I were raised in a strict home, and it was always said that "young women were meant to be seen and not heard." My parents were hard workers and ensured that food was always on the table and our basic needs were met. With the best intentions, we were always pushed to try harder and be the best. Perfection seemed to be the name of the game; if you didn't "do it" perfectly, then it appeared to not be good enough. (at least that was my perspective). There was a lot of pressure growing up "to be perfect." I believe that's where my anxiety began due to having this constant fear of failure. I was fearful of what the consequences or punishment would be if I weren't perfect. My parents had two very different styles of disciplining my sister and I. One parent was more of the passive, silent type, didn't say much, and had the superpower ability to correct poor behaviors with just a look, and we immediately knew we needed to adjust and behave appropriately.

The other parent took a more intimidating and aggressive approach (yelling, hitting, demeaning, belittling) to ensure that my sister and I followed the rules and did what we were asked to do. Despite the best intentions of either parent, I couldn't help but think/ believe "I was a disappointment," "I wasn't smart enough or would ever be good enough." As a child, all I ever wanted was to please my parents and make them proud of me. It just seemed that no matter what I did, and no matter how hard I tried, I came up short. Many people believe that in order to encourage someone to be better/ be successful, they need to be "hard" on them with the belief "the more I push you, point out your flaws/mistakes, the more you will want to improve and be your best." While that may work for some individuals, I can tell you it had the opposite effect on me. I walked away feeling disappointed, confused, sad, hopeless, and ashamed. I needed something more; I needed understanding, encouragement, and emotional support.

What is Emotional Support?

It's a verbal and/or nonverbal way to communicate with an individual by words of encouragement, reassurance, and compassion. I've learned that managing our expectations is very important in order to understand that we can't give/teach something we haven't received/learned ourselves. I don't fault my parents. No one is to blame. As a child, I had high expectations of the adults in my life and depended on them to provide me with emotional support. I expected them to have the knowledge and ability to meet ALL of my needs (Primal Needs: Food, Shelter, Love, Affection, Guidance, Protection, and Safety).

There is no denying that my parents love me. Still, there were many times in my life growing up when I didn't feel encouraged or supported, at times emotionally feeling neglected or alone, which led to me feeling sad, lonely, and like I didn't belong. I learned years later that not knowing how to communicate/express my feelings in a healthy manner led to me harboring feelings of resentment. I believed or told myself, "I am not good enough," "I am not important enough," or "I am not worthy of love."

Growing up had its mix of good times and not-so-good times. As a child and into adulthood, the not-so-good times seemed to haunt me and stand out more in my mind. My cognitive distortions or distorted perspective started at a young age. How I saw myself and others really started to leave an imprint on my mind and shaped my attitudes and behaviors, lowering my self-esteem.

What is Trauma & How it Contributes to Distorted Thinking/ Perspective?

Before I continue, it's important to understand what trauma is and how it impacts the development of the brain. Trauma is an emotional response to a distressing or disturbing experience/event. There are three types of traumas: Acute, Chronic, or Complex.

Acute Trauma results from a single incident (i.e., death of a loved one, car accident, assault). Chronic Trauma results from repeated and prolonged incidents (i.e., domestic violence, child abuse, bullying). Complex Trauma results from exposure to varied and multiple traumatic events, often of an intensive and interpersonal nature (i.e., sexual abuse, emotional neglect, and or abandonment).

In the early stages of development, when a child/adolescent experiences trauma, it has a significant impact on the development of the brain and slows down the progression of the prefrontal cortex (impairing decision making, perspectives, problem-solving skills, and ability to manage emotions). Trauma can cause your brain to remain in a state of hyper-vigilance, suppressing your memory and impulse control and trapping you in a constant state of strong emotional reactivity. As a result, individuals are more prone or have a predisposition to developing an addiction (i.e., eating disorder, gambling, sex, etc..), mental health issues (i.e., depression, anxiety, insomnia, OCD-obsessive compulsive disorder), and/or substance abuse issues (i.e., drugs/alcohol).

The Beginning of Traumatic Life Experiences

What seemed like normal life was about to change. I will share my perspective of my childhood and life experiences with you, although there are others who may disagree and have a difference of opinion or different perspective...This is my Story!

My intent in sharing my experience is to offer strength and hope with no intention to cause any harm or bring shame to anyone and their families. This is an opportunity to share how life experiences (physical abuse, sexual assault, bullying, emotional/psychological abuse, emotional neglect/abandonment) influenced me, shaping maladaptive/unhealthy attitudes and behaviors contributing to a negative perspective of self. I struggled for years with obsessive thinking, people-pleasing, and making decisions based on my emotions. It was my lack of knowledge and understanding of how unresolved trauma impacts the development of my brain that led me to believe that "there was something wrong with me, I would never be perfect, and I would never be able to make anyone happy."

My childhood trauma started with being belittled, ridiculed, bullied, and discriminated against from as early as five years old to the age of 13. By age 14, I was sexually assaulted by a friend of the family. My shame and fear suffocated me to the degree of holding in all of my feelings. Initially, I was too afraid to tell anyone what had happened. Fast forward to age 18, I felt so unworthy and believed I wasn't wanted. I desired to live life on my terms; as a result, I decided to move out of my parents' home and moved in with my boyfriend at the time, who I married a year later (A Marriage of Convenience). The following year at age 20, I suffered a miscarriage which fed into my negative beliefs as I asked myself, "what's wrong with me?" I spent all of my twenties and thirties in unhealthy/toxic relationships, sustained abuse (psychological, emotional), addiction /dependency to drugs, alcohol, and codependent relationships; all the while, my low self-esteem, depression, and anxiety issues were on the rise.

I got married at age 19 for a few reasons. Although I was young and in love, getting married would allow me to obtain legal residency in the United States and please my parents as I was reminded that the religion of Islam does not agree with a young woman cohabitating with the opposite sex prior to marriage. During the 13 years of my first marriage, I was blessed with the ability to finally be a mother of two beautiful daughters. I thought I had achieved success. I was married, had two kids, was a first-time homeowner, and was living the American dream (so I thought). I thought it was something for my parents to be proud of; however, what wasn't apparent was the emotional neglect and emotional abandonment I endured throughout the course of my marriage. My people-pleasing behaviors and fear of failure continued from childhood, and I found myself engulfed in a co-dependent relationship.

I did things to please the father of my children, and I allowed myself to endure abuse (emotionally) because I was still searching for ways to feel validated or be of value to someone. Years of abuse made it difficult for me to know what a healthy relationship was supposed to look like. My self-esteem and self-worth were nonexistent at this time in my life. My husband and I at the time indulged in mind- and mood-altering substances recreationally, and as a result, I was so far removed from being in a relationship with GOD that seeking GOD for help/guidance was not a thought I entertained.

I was raised in a home where GOD was a constant presence; however, being mistreated and sexually assaulted and bullied as a child led me to be so angry with GOD that I turned my back on him (not a moment in time I was proud of and had to ask for forgiveness). As a result of not keeping GOD at the center of my life, and spending most of my time up until that point trying to control every aspect of my life, my husband and I grew apart in the relationship. After 13 years of marriage, my children's father had an affair, filed for divorce, and sought primary custody of our children. The courts deemed my children's father more capable of providing stability because he and his new girlfriend were a two-person household that could provide 9-5 stability, whereas I was a single mother working odd hours and incapable of providing stability to my children.

Losing my marriage and my children "was the straw that broke the camel's back." I began to use drugs and alcohol more frequently. My children's father and I used drugs and alcohol socially (consumed alcohol, smoked marijuana), and over the course of our marriage, we progressed to being high-functioning users. We maintained our home, jobs and raised our children to the best of our ability. Due to no consequences of our use of mind- and mood-altering substances, we were both in denial that our use was problematic to our children and ourselves. While we (justified our behaviors) by not using mind- and mood-altering substances in front of our children, they suffered emotional neglect. As a result of the divorce and losing custody of my daughters, they also suffered abandonment issues.

By age 30, I was distraught and exhausted from trying to be a people-pleaser, problem solver, fixer, and martyr. I wound up feeling defeated, re-affirming earlier childhood beliefs that I am a failure and was not worthy and deserving of good things, which led to my suicide attempt. This was a turning point in my life. The buried guilt, shame, disappointment, fear, and every negative belief and suppressed emotion I held onto as a child erupted inside of me, causing me to give up. Being self-centered and thinking only of me at the time, I wanted to die and leave my children behind, thinking and believing that they deserved better and would live a better life without me in it...like I said, how self-centered of me (another moment in time I am not proud of). I hope my experiences showcase why I spent living my life in fear, shame/guilt, and bondage because I didn't know how to rise from the ashes that were my life.

My narrative up until this point was "I am a victim;" therefore, I wasn't fierce. I was timid; I wasn't fabulous- I was ordinary/small and insignificant, and I certainly wasn't free. I remained in bondage/ trapped in my mind and was constantly reminded of my weaknesses and failures. Up until this point, I acted like I was a higher power, believing I was in control of everyone and every circumstance. Yet, internally, I was feeling helpless, hopeless, and powerless. I struggled to ask for help due to pride and an inflated ego. I lacked healthy coping skills, didn't know how to communicate in a healthy manner, and didn't even know how I was feeling or what I needed. But I am a big believer that GOD allows people to cross our paths for specific reasons, sometimes for a season or in some instances a lifetime. GOD knows exactly what we need and when we need it, even if we have no clue.

How My Higher Power Created Me to Be Fierce, Fabulous & Free!

In December 2008, I had undergone surgery and had a partial hysterectomy at the age of 29. According to the reports of the physician, during surgery, I had endured a torn pelvis, which caused an internal bleed. As a result, my blood pressure dropped, and I flatlined briefly. Following surgery, I was hospitalized for almost a week, and then I returned to my home to continue with the recovery process. Little did I know this would be a turning point in my life.

During this time, I was in the middle of my divorce and the custody battle I mentioned earlier. I returned to an empty apartment that was no longer full of life, as my daughters needed to stay with their father until I recovered. The first few days, I was exhausted and weak, so I slept most of the time, but as I slowly began to spend more time awake, I found myself alone with just myself and my "unhealthy/distorted" thoughts... again!

My mental state was unhealthy due to years of addiction, enduring multiple forms of abuse, and now dealing with the grief and loss of my family – failed marriage, and losing my children. I was living in Texas at the time, and my family lived in Florida and were not within reach for the comfort and support I needed, and I didn't have anyone that I could lean on. This was a defining moment and what I considered "my rock bottom" (I had lost my house in Florida, in the process of losing my 13-year marriage, losing my daughters, and now my health was deteriorating).

As I looked around the room, I began to feel great despair. I began to experience anxiety and overwhelming sadness of the person I had become (a complete failure) that contributed to my severe state of depression. I was reminded then, and still to this day, that I can find comfort in the following scripture, Jeremiah 29:11, *"For I know the plans I have for you, declares the Lord, to prosper you and not to harm you, to give you hope and a future."* GOD knew exactly what he was doing as he guided me and carried me through that period in my life, opening my eyes, ears, and heart to embrace what I like to call "GOD moments."

GOD MOMENTS

A week or two after being at home trying to heal my physical body, I received a phone call from an individual who I met through a work conference approximately one year before. This individual called me one day and expressed that he had learned I was ill and wanted to pray for me. At the time, I was completely blocked from GOD and denied that a "Higher Power" existed due to the life I had endured up until that point and was very resentful. I would like to refer to this individual as my "guardian angel." He called me daily to read a verse out of the Bible and then told me, "Keep your head above water," they would hang up with no expectation in return. My "Guardian Angel" called me at the same time every day and shared the word of GOD with me for seven days in a row. A month into the recovery process, GOD anointed me with another angel, an old friend that I knew since the sixth grade, who heard that I wasn't doing well, and she came to visit.

She stayed in my living room on the sofa for three days and prayed for me without ceasing. We didn't have much conversation and I believe wholeheartedly that she prayed for a new life in me. Six weeks into recovery I began to walk again, and I began to start feeling the spirit of GOD within me. I began to feel alive (FREE) and rejuvenated in a way I can't really put into words or explain sometimes.

I was ready to return to work, and I was ready to face and fight any battles that lay ahead (i.e., my divorce).
I was ready to start a new life.

I believe that my higher power (GOD) was with me the entire time during that 8-week period, and even in times before, despite what

I had been through, he was always with me. I chose to walk away from GOD. A client once told me, "God is a gentleman. He is always with us, but he would not enter our space/circumstances if we don't seek Him first and seek his help and guidance." Isaiah 43: 1-3, *"Do not be afraid for I have ransomed you. I have called you by name, you are mine when you go through deep waters, I will be with you when you go through rivers of difficulty; you will not drown when you walk through the fire of oppression, you will not be buried up, the flames will not consume you for I am the Lord your GOD."*

GOD wasn't just healing my physical being but also my mental and spiritual being; I believe today that I am a spiritual being navigating a human experience rather than a human being seeking a spiritual experience. I am reminded of 2 Peter 3:9, *"Trust in the Lord with all your heart and do not lean on your own understanding. In all your ways, acknowledge him, and he will make straight your paths."* So April 2009, at the age of 31, I made the decision to surrender my will (need to control) and sought a closer, more meaningful relationship with GOD.

That same year, I returned to the sunshine state of South Florida, my hometown of Delray Beach, and began a new life in recovery, without my spouse, without my children, and without an identity. I was given the opportunity for a new beginning and the chance to re-write my narrative. At the age of 31, I was no longer defined by the role of being a wife or a mother. I didn't know who I was, but GOD knew and provided me with the spiritual strength and internal fortitude to not give up and to begin my search for meaning and discover my authentic self in my recovery journey. Because of GOD's unconditional love, grace, mercy, and forgiveness, my continued spiritual walk, my undeniable faith and trust in GOD, Today I **am Fierce**– I have regained the power in my voice to speak my truth, **I am Fabulous**– no longer ordinary but a force to be reckoned with. I am a child of GOD, and **I am Free**– free from bondage, free from abuse, free to be unapologetically me, free to love and be loved. Today, I love myself and get to love others the same way GOD has shown me with unconditional love. 1 Corinthians 13:4-7, *"Love is patient, kind, it does not envy, it does not boast, it is not proud, it is not rude, it is not self-seeking, it is not easily angered, keeps no record of wrong, does not delight in evil, rejoices with the truth, always protects, trust, hopes, perseveres and never fails."*

GOD has restored my vision, and through a new pair of lenses, I am no longer a victim, I am Victorious! The day I chose to surrender my will and let go of control and the desire to live by my rules and what I want was the day my life changed. The 12-step program of Alcoholics Anonymous, my sponsor, mentors, spiritual leaders, empowered women, and continuing to seek GOD allows me to have a free spirit, a fierce voice, and a fabulous mind. I am blessed and called to empower the voices of others who have endured trauma to rise from the ashes, let GOD mend your broken heart, release your pain and tell your story, share your experiences, providing strength and hope to others. It will change and save a life! My trials and tribulations have paved the way for me to grow in a closer relationship with God and to walk by faith, not by sight.

(2 Corinthian 5:7)

DAILY REFLECTION

"Transformation begins with seeing things from a different perspective."

36.

Biography

Natashah Khan was born and raised in the Caribbean Island of Trinidad and Tobago. Natashah is a therapist by trade but her primary focus is being an Educator, Published Author, Personal Development Coach; also an Advocate for Change by increasing Awareness on Addiction, and removing the STIGMA in our society and helping others learn how to embrace the challenges they face while learning how to emotionally heal from the negative impact of addiction. Natashah is a motivational speaker, Empowering Women, empowering the voices of those silenced due to abuse, (physical, sexual, emotional, psychological), neglect, (emotional or physical), abandonment, (emotional or physical), and unresolved trauma they may have endured over their lifetime. Natashah has earned a master's degree in Counseling Psychology, graduating Cum Laude; along with a bachelor's degree in Business Mgt, graduating with honors. Natashah's areas of expertise are substance abuse, treating dual diagnosis patients in an inpatient

Mental Health setting for over two decades. Additionally for the last five years Natashah has built a platform for families to share their emotional and mental suffering; while empowering their voices through her weekly online support group and 1:1 personal development coaching sessions, in efforts to provide healing, spiritual guidance and empower others to begin living their purpose driven life. She is also the Sole Developer & Facilitator of a Family Healing Retreat (3-day Seminar) focusing on familial relationships & her client's relationship dynamics with their partners, their families, & individuals.

PASSION: Natashah has dedicated her time in healing relationships and is a published Author of 2 Virtual Articles- Understanding the Disease of Addiction and Victim to Victory; she is also, a contributing writer for a virtual magazine- I Shine Magazine

GOAL: Having been a survivor of Abuse and in Recovery for the last 11 years Natashah has established EMPOWERED VOICES LLC- where she is a Relational Coach focusing on Empowering others to have a voice, fulfill their life's purpose and to heal from the wounds that have become disruptive and hindered their ability to live their lives in a fulfilling and meaningful way.

XIII

Rhonda Williams-Turner

37.

Dedication

GOD- Thank you for covering me and blessing me!

This book is dedicated to my family. Thank you for being who you are. Without all the ups and the downs, I would not have become the strong woman I am today! With it all being said, Evelyn Lawrence, I dedicate myself to you always. Although you are not here on earth, you mold me into this empowering woman that empowers others. I will keep pushing because you taught me to continue no matter how hard the road may be… take a turn and get on another road and make it your success. I love you forever and always.

38.

The Experience

As I sit here humbled and thankful to be a part of the I AM A Woman Empowered Anthology, Volume 2, I was thinking about what it means to me to be Fierce, Fabulous, and Free. At first, I was hesitant because I thought, am I ready for volume 2? Am I qualified to be with so many amazing women? Then I became nervous because I feared that with all I have going on, will I be committed or have the time, etc.? Then, my emotions shifted to honor because, once again, someone thought so highly of me that they would even ask or let me be a part of this amazing journey. Despite all that, the real issue was why did I believe that I did not deserve it? More specifically, why didn't I believe in myself? Too often, as women, we do this to ourselves. Why should I think that it's not for me? I contemplated if it was because of the decisions that I made in the early part of my life that made me feel less than, coupled with other people speaking negatively towards me and negatively over my life. Many times that is what people do; they create toxic surroundings because of their unhappiness. It seems as if they are not happy with their own lives, so they decide to make others unhappy or miserable.

As I prepared to write my chapter, I went back and forth about what I would say. How theoretical and analytical I would be, or how motivational or empowering would my chapter seem. I decided to write what I know from the heart because it's me and things I have experienced. Every experience in my life was orchestrated to teach me something and show me what I need to know to move forward—understanding that the only source of knowledge is my own experience.

Women do not want to hear the same thing about motivating, encouraging, and how to survive out here in this world we call ours. Women want and desire more. So, I will try and keep it basic. I reverted to what I know and to what motivates me daily. What can I say about Fierce, Fabulous and Free?

Why FIERCE?

Fierce is defined as being menacingly wild, savage, or hostile. There is no fear in fierce. Wild does not have to mean being out of control but can mean being fierce with force, strength, and determination. To be fierce is known as an attitude. It is a way of living your life with little reservation or hesitation. We were given this life because we are strong enough to live it. Why apologize for who you are? God created you; there is a purpose in you.

It is always good to be strong. You never know who you are inspiring or leading from a distance—becoming that woman who wakes up each day and takes the world on—not caring what's about to get in her way, only caring that she takes it on as strong and mighty as she can be. It is okay to look in the mirror and see your own flaws and not point out the flaws of others around you. Do you say, "I'm beautiful just the way I am," and know that inside and out? Are you that woman juggling a career while married with children and doing it well? That is real and makes you feel empowered. Are you a woman who fights for what's right, takes a stand for what she believes, and doesn't feel the need to explain herself to anyone?

Being fierce, you become that woman. Remember to embrace who you are every day and love yourself fiercely! We live in a world where too many people judge others and where we are too hard on ourselves. Yet, when you're a woman who is secure in who you are, that's the moment you know you're on top. At that moment, you keep building yourself up while building other women up around you. Every day you wake up, your challenge is to find what is fierce about you and use it to motivate you and push you through your day to be better and go after it. As a FIERCE woman, you are not a difficult woman; you are a strong woman that knows her worth.

Example of a fierce woman:

Take the women in slavery. They were fierce women… when the master took them from their families and made them house slaves, he tried to break them down. He had no respect for the black family. Because the woman knew she had to hold her family together by sleeping with the enemy, she dealt with her lot in life. It is good to know when and how to be strong enough to stand alone and how to be smart enough to know who you need to stand with and how to be brave enough to ask. That is called a fierce black woman.

Why FABULOUS?

A fabulous woman knows how to be charismatic in all situations, building confidence within yourself to be able to handle a situation with grace and mercy. To be fabulous is the combination of your outward appearance and your inner spirit. It is important to take pride in how you appear to others. Being a fabulous woman is being the type of woman that can smooth over any unfriendly situation, promoting more positivity and togetherness. Knowing that you are a cultivated woman means you are a refined and well-educated woman. It can exist to help women become spiritually wise, relationally kind, emotionally healthy, and connected in one's community serving together as a team. It is a place where you are challenged to be real with yourself, God, and others. You, as a woman, are fearfully and wonderfully made.

"I praise you because I am fearfully and wonderfully made; your work is wonderful; I know that full well." Psalms 139:14

As a fabulous woman, God made all the delicate inner parts of you and your body. He knit us all together within our mother's womb. We all were made wonderfully complex. God knew you as he formed and designed you with much loving and tender care. You just don't evolve into what you are. You are created and designed with a purpose. You may have a blueprint, but no one is the same. YOU ARE UNIQUE!

No one can do what you can do. They may try but what you do is unique in its own way. Sometimes that can be good, and sometimes no one wants to do it your way because they feel it is not done correctly. It is important to understand that you are who you are because God created you, not man. His desire for you to be a strong person is who he is. A fabulous person can come in many shapes and sizes. As a fabulous person, you have the ability to have discernment and understand right from wrong situations.

We were not designed to do our own things (wrong things), but as humans, we sometimes choose to be defiant and do things that may not be of GOD. One thing we must say, we were designed with an intense need of the Creator, God. Without a relationship with Him, you will always be searching for something to fill that void. Drugs, alcohol, food, money, sex, material goods, occupations, hobbies, travel, success, fame—these are some of the ways in which we try to fill that empty space inside. But none of those things will ever fill it. Sadly, many continue to shove mismatched pegs into that hole. A little of this, a little of that... hoping that they will feel complete one day, which they believe makes them fabulous.

Here are some things that we may say that we believe will complete us:

One day...

- I'll have enough money to feel safe and travel the world because I am secure.

- I'll find the perfect spouse that will complete me, and we will live happily ever after.
- I'll be famous, and people will know my name.
- I'll be the best at what I do, and people will choose me over others.

"One day" will never come. If you're not happy with who you are today, right here and right now, you'll never be.

We all have weaknesses that sometimes make us feel like we are useless. But God's grace is sufficient to cover our shortcomings and make us fabulous. More than that, God's power is made perfect in our weakness. Weaknesses keep me humble and leaning on God's strength which is much more sufficient than my own. This is something many may not be able to see, but due to life situations, you learn how to depend on him. People will try and take your power, and it is up to you not to give it to them. Be intentional about being fabulous. Understand that God made you, and there is nothing anyone can do about it.

A person will always be prejudged, and far too often, you will not get a second chance to make a great impression. Put your best foot forward. Invest in yourself and be a fabulous person. To truly be incredibly fabulous, you must believe in who you are! Make yourself a priority, and your walk will be exceptional that others may see who you are and remember that GOD created you and that GOD does not make any junk! Take your power back and become FABULOUS within yourself. Be proud of the woman you have become because most of the time, you have to go through hell to be her.

NOW TO BE FREE!

Sometimes, the thing you were afraid of doing is the very thing that will set you free. Over time, you will learn that we are so afraid of the next steps, and those steps can lead you in the right direction called freedom. Nothing is better than a woman who knows what she wants and understands how to get it. It is good to appreciate people's opinions but do not let them take your power... when you give them the power to feed you, it gives them the power to starve you too. Learn that people have motives, and most of the time, their motives are not for you or your dreams to survive. What he created for you may not be for those that may be intimidated by you. Sometimes you may have to leave being normal behind to be free.

Maya Angelou stated:

A woman in harmony with her spirit is like a river flowing. She goes where she will without pretense and arrives at her destination prepared to be herself and only herself. – Maya Angelou

The best thing for a free woman is to love yourself, be yourself, and shine bright like the diamond you are. What is a DIAMOND? Part of that definition is a diamond is a solid form. It has the highest hardness of any natural material. The most important part of that is a diamond is known for its outstanding brilliance and fire. You are the diamond that is unbreakable and free. A powerful woman knows how to dust herself off and shine bright like a diamond, even after the worst has happened. Stop moaning and groaning about what you could have done or what someone did to you, and that is why you can't. Turn your I can't into I did.

You are a DIAMOND dear. They can't break you. Let no one stop your freedom or rob you of your peace. You are a woman that is amazing, strong, and most of all free, so don't get caught in that negative trap that we call what others may say or feel. Never apologize for being a powerful free woman. Take what you have and use it to create your freedom by staying focused and making it happen. Life has rules but do not let it cripple you and stop you from breathing the right air. Check your attitude because bad behavior can push you in the wrong direction. They say women don't have attitudes; they have standards (LOL). Focus on being free; it always seems impossible until it is done. Most of the time, we cannot see the path that is provided, so we start thinking negatively and start speaking negatively over ourselves. Remember the words you speak out of your mouth can direct your path.

The tongue has the power of life and death. Proverbs 18-21.

THE MESSAGE IS IN YOUR MOUTH! BE MINDFUL! TASTE THEM BEFORE SPITTING THEM OUT…

Do not ever stop believing in yourself. When in doubt, hit the auto-correct, rewrite and know your value. We, as women, are fearful and not living our dreams. We are walking on eggshells to become who we desire to be. A woman should have that free spirit that when asked where you are going, the woman can answer, "I am going in the right DIRECTION! Realize the strength you have, discover the abilities God gave you, and uncover how powerful you are as a woman.

You are a beautiful woman. OWN IT… because your freedom belongs to you. Remember, the DREAM is FREE; the HUSTLE is sold separately.

"A wise woman builds," Proverbs 14:1.

As a woman, be open to change; you never know just how free you can be!

In Closing

Push harder today than you did yesterday if you desire a better tomorrow. Don't worry about seeking revenge. Move and let God handle your lightweight. Make sure your circle is small because I am about the quality and not the quantity. You are who you are, and others' approval is not needed. Life grows in the proportion of one's courage. Do you have the courage to be free? If yes, create your steps and follow your path. God gives us hope which has everything. Success is the best revenge. Let success direct you to that freedom.

There is always something special about a woman who may overcome obstacles that try and destroy her, but it can't because the bible verse says: "I can do all things through CHRIST who strengthens me." – Philippians 4:13. So create your own revolution! At any given time, you, as a Fierce, Fabulous, and Free woman, can say this is not how the story will end. On any day, in any situation, you can choose to be… Fierce, Fabulous, and most of all, Free!

39.

Biography

Rhonda Williams-Turner has been a role model, mentor, and community leader in the community of Palm Beach County for over 25 years. She is married to an amazing man, Mr. Turner, for 23+ years, and she has five children, four sons, and a daughter.

Mrs. Turner is the founder of 4 Knowledge is Power, a nonprofit, and holds a master's degree in Mental Health and Marriage & Family. She has faithfully worked to implement numerous youth and adults' programs and events. She seeks to positively influence and empower today's youth with the understanding that the formative years are the most critical years to make the biggest impact for transformative change. 4 Knowledge Is Power encourages a positive education not only through books but also through learning African American history. For the past 19 years, she has taken high school students around the United States to numerous Colleges and Historical Tours.

Mrs. Turner utilizes her Master of Science degree in Mental Health and Marriage & Family to empower women and highlight local black marriages through a host of events. Mrs. Turner has built a legacy that has grown over many years in leadership and commitment within her community.

One of Mrs. Turner's mottos is Dream Bigger, Reach Higher and Achieve More. Become that leader you expect others to be!

Quote for this year:

"It's time for you to move, realizing that the thing you are seeking is also seeking you." — Iyanla Vanzant

XIV
Tammie Parker

40.

Dedication

I would like to dedicate this book to my husband- Derrick Parker. For always having patience with me, praying for me, and never leaving. You have seen me at my worst, and you still love me. To my kids~ you guys are the reason I go so hard! To my grandbabies – cause you all think I'm a SUPERHERO to you! To my mom for always encouraging me! To all the other women out there who refuse to give up.

41.

Free To Be Me!

Here I am! 50 years old, and standing in GODS GRACE! Reflecting on ALL that GOD has brought me through. I remember being so broken and depressed. Even asking GOD to take me out of the misery I felt. Unable to release the pain from a childhood of rejection, hurt, and abandonment, I was LOST! Always in my head. Trying to see where I fit in. I didn't trust anyone... not even myself. God had put so many things inside me that I know he wanted to bring out. He told me by gifts are not for me, but to bless others. And yet here I was STUCK! Confused about how to proceed. Living in frustration – sitting in the background while I watched other people LIVE OUT THEIR DREAMS! My body ached from all of the things swirling around in my mind. Everything looked perfect on the outside. I could dress up really pretty, put on the best perfume, and muster up a smile. I could encourage others, go out of my way to help them, and stand in the gap for them. I put everything and everyone else in front of my needs. I had a wonderful husband. My kids are all grown and doing ok. Beautiful grandchildren. I was blessed with a brand new home, a job that provided finances. I have good friends and people who genuinely love me. So why was I questioning myself? Why did I feel so unworthy? Because I knew that I was blessed, so why did I not FEEL like it. I felt pressure, to look perfect, and be good... thought I was screaming inside. I was desperate- and finally CRIED OUT TO GOD WHHYYYY!!! Every area of my life was in turmoil. I convinced myself that my family didn't love me. I was devastated because I lost friends that I had for years the people that I could confide in- GONE! My health had begun to fail from all the mental stress.

The GOD told me to LOOK! DIGG DEEP! Look at you- really look at you. Are you being your authentic self? Are you doing what it is you want to do? Are you thankful for what you have? And have you really, really forgiven? He told me you have to be REAL! You have to be GRATEFUL!

There is where I had to begin the hard work. Get to the ROOT of why I was struggling so much. I did just as God instructed. I began to DIG. I found the scars emotional and mental scars from my childhood. Being raised in the dysfunction of a drug-addicted mother, who choose to leave me at 12 with the man who molested me. Facing rejection I felt when my father moved on to the next marriage and forgot about me. Fighting with the spiritual residue of all the men that I allow to be with me just so I would feel loved. I had to deal with all the fact that I was exhausted from working two, even sometimes three jobs to make ends meet for the two daughters that came from my promiscuity. Not to mention mistakes I made trying to figure out how to be the best mom to them that I could be. Fending for myself most of the time. This made me put up a SHIELD. I told myself I would not let anyone else control how I lived anymore. Never expected anything but abandonment and let down from anyone who was supposed to love and protect me. I would do whatever it took to show my kids that they had a safe place. I would be there with them and for them. And that wasn't all.

These experiences also made me feel as though I didn't fit in. I was always the one with no support, no real friends, not a part of the click. People always looked at me as being something totally different than what I truly am. From the time I was in middle school, living in public housing. I can remember being bullied by the girls I wanted so badly to have friendships with. Because they saw the name-brand clothes I wore. They just assumed I thought I was better, but in reality, I was going through hell at home. On through my adult life, until recently, I still felt like I was not invited- not a part of the click- not part of the in-crowd. Not having any close friends that I could really let in. Looked at as the STRONG one- I was cracking.

Still digging up STUFF- Now I'm married. And here we are together. I had my stuff- and he had his. Trying to figure out how to be a "good wife" to the man that God had sent to me. Our marriage was hit from all sides. My husband was laid off from his job of 25 years after the company eliminated his position. We lost our house and car. My husband, in his struggle to keep his masculine image- totally shut me out. As he tried to process what was going on within his own mind, he didn't realize that he was showing me everything that I saw throughout my life. He had abandoned me emotionally. Now I built another fence- to shield me from the very person I should share my most intimate self with. This was more trauma- piled on top of everything else I was carrying. The stench from all the emotional deaths that had taken place in my life was really bad. The weight of all this made me feel so heavy. My youth was gone, my health was failing- so it made me question if physical death would be better for me. I had no JOY, I was TIRED!

OK, GOD! I can't do this anymore! Will I know what it feels like to just be at PEACE? Not have to work so hard! Would I get to a place where I would be able to tear down these fences I built to protect me- that are now caving in on me? To just be accepted for just who I am? To have real loving friendships? To have a life with some JOY? And you know what GOD said... I love you unconditionally! I love you more than your earthly mother and father. Even in those times that you felt so vulnerable, I was protecting you. He showed me the purpose of feeling like an outsider- I can't walk with everyone. The treasure- in the gifts he had stored within me was too valuable. He told me that I was making things harder on myself because I had not done what he said in his word- GIVE HIM MY BURDENS TO BARE! I don't have to be STRONG all the time. Only strong in him.

I LISTENED! I gave it all to GOD. My issues, my worries, my problems, my cares. I promised to love him FIRST! I became intentional with actions, my thought, and words. I started praying consistently. Not only to tell God my desires, but for direction in every area of my life. I lean totally on him. Doing this has given me peace that I could not have ever imagined.

I also realized that I was so distracted with all the turmoil that I had going on within me, I was missing the things that God wanted me to do. I had so many gifts and blessings that the world would miss if I don't submit to my calling in him. So each day on purpose, my goal is to do what he has instructed me for that day... Because he has given me GRACE for that. Stop over thinking it, keep it simple and MOVE when he says.

HIS STRENGTH! That is what has carried me, what steadies me. I realized these things:

I am FIRECE- because the POWER that I possess comes from the Lord! I can do nothing without him. I'm equip with his graces and mercy to make it through anything that comes my way!

I am Fabulous- because I am made in God's image. I'm not perfect, but I am beautiful in his eyes. I strive to be a carrier of his light, integrity, and love, so that his GLORY is what the world will see despite my multitude of flaws.

I AM FREE!! – because I have laid down everything that weighs me down- depression, anxiety, hurt, fear, doubt, confusion, lack, and anger at his feet. I lean on God totally to fight my battles. I BELIEVE what his word says about me! THANK GOD FOR FREEDOM!

42.

Biography

Tammie Parker is a wife, mother, and the owner of Coco's Soulfood Kitchen Catering LLC. Her passion is serving GOD by helping others, cooking, and spending time with friends. She enjoys traveling and meeting new people. Her mission in life is to Please God and all that she does!

XV

Angela Lewis

43.

Dedication

To my husband, Dewayne, and my daughters, Alexis and Alonna: Thank you for your love and support. It always has been and always will be about the three of you!

To the ladies who decided to join me on this journey: Thank you for your transparency and willingness to be fierce, fabulous, and free together!

44.

Living my Life Unmuted

As children, we were the epitome of fierce, fabulous, and free. We embraced life fully, never questioning if we could do things; we knew we could, so we did. We were inquisitive and fearless, without a care in the world. However, over time we became muted without even realizing it. We heard the words "Shutup" or "Be Quiet" more frequently, sprinkled with a liberal dose of "No!" We were told, "Stop talking so much," and "Children should be seen and not heard." Yet, the one that sealed the deal was, "What goes on in this house stays in this house."

That phrase set the precedence of never telling. It became difficult and uncomfortable to speak our truth or tell our story from that point on. You were labeled a tattle-tale in school if you spoke up about things. Even as adults, phrases like snitches got stitches reflected a universal code of silence that most people adhered to. It seemed easier to ignore the truth and stay quiet.

However, contrary to what people think, it costs us more to stay quiet than it does for us to speak up. Oprah Winfrey said, "What I know for sure is that speaking your truth is the most powerful tool we have." We all have a story to tell, a message to share, or a simple thought to be heard. It is through our voice- our story- that we can connect ourselves to the world around us. When we don't speak up for ourselves, we break down our sense of self-worth. When we give up our voice, we mask our true identity and diminish our uniqueness.

We are afraid to speak up because we are afraid to alienate others.

Yet, when we don't speak our truth, we actually end up alienating ourselves. We go into a downward spiral of anxiety, depression, and sometimes even suicidal thoughts. Recently, Miss USA 2019, Chelsie Krist, tragically committed suicide. Her mother said she suffered from high functioning depression, and she had no idea Chelsie was at such a low point in her life.

Another reason we don't speak up is we believe expressing our opinion may lead to criticism or ridicule, or we believe our opinion is not valued. We think we will be rejected, judged, retaliated against, or diminished in some way. Instead, we stay quiet, dumb down, or play small, anticipating nothing will happen if we speak up or we won't be believed.

For me, I grew up a talker. I'm a preacher's kid, so I guess I got it honest. In school, I would always be in time out or have to write 100 or more times, "I will not talk in class." In spite of the talking, I was really good in my studies, taking advanced classes and excelling with my grades. However, I went to a predominately white school, and the people who were in those classes didn't look like me. I began to talk less and less. I felt socially awkward because I wasn't in their circle.

Since I didn't fit in there, I wanted to fit in at other places. I became a people pleaser and didn't feel confident, even when I knew I was more intelligent or had the correct answers. When it came to dating, I would see red flags, but I chose to ignore them. I went so far as to marry someone I knew was cheating on me. I didn't want to speak my truth because I was embarrassed. I didn't want to tell anyone what was going on because I didn't want to be judged, so I tried to make the best of it.

My decision to be silent led to the failure of my marriage, no confidence, and low self-esteem. As I dealt with my failed marriage, I was also trying to cope with being a single mother. In the midst of that, my father died. Three years later, my mother passed and several years after that, so did my sister. I was mute about my pain, but the grief was overwhelming! However, in 2020, I found my voice in the midst of a pandemic, and I was ready to tell my story.

I didn't want to tell it alone, so I invited others to come along on the journey. That year 24 ladies and I wrote an anthology, "I Am a Woman Empowered: Stories of Strength, Resiliency, and Triumphs. We used our voices, and we told our stories. I began to find my confidence. I began to feel bold. Yet, years of not speaking my truth and holding in my pain led to high blood pressure, high cholesterol, and eventually diabetes. I did not learn about the latter until I had a mini-stroke in March of 2021.

I had to re-evaluate my life and say, "ENOUGH IS ENOUGH!" I had to speak my truth and get rid of the things that no longer served me. I knew my worth, and it was time for me to start adding tax! In August 2021, I turned in my two-week notice at the job and never looked back. Like a butterfly in a cocoon, I was ready to emerge Fierce, Fabulous, and Free. I was ready to truly live my life unmuted.

In being Fierce, I realized my voice was powerful. Our voice is our expression of power, and we are powerful beyond measure. Our story, our voice, has the power to connect people to a shared experience that makes them feel less alone in the world and gives them the strength to want to do better and be better. This is the season to be fierce and speak your truth -unleash the power of your voice.

In being Fabulous, I understood my voice matters. No two voices are the same. Each voice has something different to say. Know that what you have to say is of value. Your voice gives your opinions a platform to speak on things of importance. Through our voice, we are fabulous and unique. We have the ability to shake things up and champion causes we believe in.

In being Free, I recognized my voice inspires change. When you find the courage to speak your truth, it has the power to positively make a difference and inspire change in the lives of others. What we go through happens to us, but it's not always for us. Our voice is our superpower; it liberates us.

As we speak up and share our truth, we become a light for others. In my favorite poem by Marianne Williamson, "Our Deepest Fear," she says, "As we let our light shine, we unconsciously give other people permission to do the same. As we are liberated from our own fear, our presence automatically liberates others."

Former Secretary of State, Madeline Albright, said, "It took me quite a long while to develop a voice, and now that I have it, I'm not going to be silent." Your voice is powerful—your voice matters. Your voice inspires change. On the other side of fear lies your greatest opportunity for growth. It is time to live your life unmuted and become Fierce, Fabulous, and Free!

45.

Biography

Angela "ALove" Lewis is an Empowerment Speaker, Visibility Coach, and Publisher residing in the metro Atlanta area. Passionate about helping women use their gifts, talents, and voice, Angela guides their brands with proven strategies that provide the visibility and credibility needed for them to "Elevate and Dominate" in the marketplace.

Her desire to give women a voice and see them share their personal stories to empower others was the catalyst behind her anthology, "I Am a Woman Empowered: Stories of Strength, Resiliency & Triumphs." Since publishing the book, Angela has assisted numerous others in publishing their work through her company, A & M Publishing & Productions. She is editor-in-chief of the digital magazine iShine Magazine, a curated publication designed to showcase individuals making an impact in the community. In addition, Angela hosts two podcasts, iShine Podcast, and InnerVation: Motivating You From the Inside Out.

She believes everyone has a story to tell and should be free to speak their truth and live their life UNMUTED. Your voice has power; your voice matters; and your voice inspires change! If you are ready to speak up and share your story, connect with Angela @iamangelalewis on all social media platforms or via her website at www.iamangelalewis.com.